BASIC RECIPES FROM COPENHAGEN

ICE CREAM
According to Østerberg

new Heroes & Pioneers

MY BIGGEST GRATITUDE GOES TO

PERSONALLY

My parents Vibeke & Niels, for being you: the strongest and most supportive people I know. You have in your own individual and special ways taught me the most important lessons in life and provided me with all the opportunities to make this ice cream journey happen. Thank you!

ACADEMICALLY

Professor Douglas Goff, University of Guelph, for sharing your knowledge and expertise in the field of ice cream science with me.

Published by New Heroes & Pioneers

Text and recipes: Cathrine Østerberg
Photography: Daniel Zachrisson
Creative Direction: Francois Le Bled
Book Design: Daniel Zachrisson
Copy Editing: Matt Porter

Print and bound by AS Printon (Estonia)
Legal Deposit July 2019
ISBN 978-91-87815-61-4

Copyright 2019 New Heroes & Pioneers. All rights reserved.
Reproduction in whole or in part is prohibited without the authorisation of the publisher and the photographer.

Appearing in the book: Cathrine Østerberg, Marie-Louise Søgaard, Matilde Urbano

Contents

	Preface	5
	Background	6
	Need to know	8
	Definitions	12
	Nice to know	14
BASE & SYRUP	Ice cream bases	18
	Sorbet syrups	22
RECIPES	Ice cream & sorbet	26
	Brownie	94
	Salty caramel	95
	Nougat	97
	Cookie dough	99
	Cookies	102
	Nut paste	104
	Fruit sauce	107
	Cones	108
	Sticks	111
	Melting chocolate	112
	Cakes	114
SCIENCE	Ingredients	119
	Production	128
	Structure	130
	Sugar & scoopability	135
	Want to know	138
	Index of recipes	142
	Conversion table	143
	References & special thanks	144

Preface

Some of my very first childhood memories include ice creams and the many talks our family had during after-dinner walks with ice creams in our hands. The ultimate feeling of "hygge".

Besides ice cream, I have always loved baking and cooking, so when I found out there was a degree called food science, I knew I had found my calling in life. When the first lectures on ice cream science appeared, my mind started to become full with ideas and it felt like pieces in a puzzle starting to fall into place. The underlying mechanisms involved in creating creamy, delicious ice creams and sorbets were based on a combination of maths, physics and chemistry. My favourite courses in school since I was a teenager. No need to say that this was the perfect match for me: science made delicious and useful!

This book is first of all an ice cream recipe book. However, it is not just for fun, it says "according to Østerberg" on the cover. No doubt the recipes are great on their own, but understanding the science is where some of the real fun begins. It is like looking under the water to see more than just the tip of the iceberg. The book has been built up in such a way that you are presented with the recipes first and then you can read all about the science afterwards. In this way, you can start by making the recipes. Hopefully you will become so curious that you will want to find out how the structures are developed and how the recipes are built up that you cannot stop yourself from reading the rest of the book.

The recipes have been developed so they have the best fit for small-scale household machines to ensure the smoothest ice creams and sorbets possible for you at home. I sincerely hope you will try to produce a lot of the recipes, use the knowledge to develop more recipes and create some fantastic ice cream memories for yourself and your loved ones.

Because to me that is what ice cream is all about – happiness.

Without further ado, I hope you will enjoy making, eating and learning about ice cream.

— Cathrine Østerberg

Background

When people ask me what I do for a living, I usually say I am an ice cream girl. Here is my path to becoming that 'ice cream girl'.

There might be a very obvious reason for my big interest in food: the majority of our family dinner conversations were influenced by my father's work. He (Niels Østerberg) has a fruit manufacturing business, Orana. I remember hearing about so many exotic fruits like tamarind, mangosteen and the many different kinds of mangoes that he was sourcing from around the world. That was as natural to talk about as the raspberries and strawberries we know so well here in Denmark. Alongside this, I also heard about the challenges that came with having businesses around the world. Sometimes I was lucky enough to travel with him, which presented the opportunity of tasting the most delicious fruits from all over the world.

When I was 13 I was told to find a job. I could not think of a better place to work than the local ice cream parlour. Everybody told me I would get sick and tired of ice cream after one summer as an ice cream girl. On the contrary, I was intrigued by the different textures, flavour pairings and seeing the joy on people's faces when they got their ice creams.

Before opening the first ice cream shop, I thought long and hard of how to stand out from all other ice cream shops. The answer was so obvious: I wanted to offer our customers some of the amazing fruits and ingredients from all over the world that could not be typically found in other parlours. So, I have done just that and combined my father's expertise in the fruit business and my knowledge in the ice cream field.

This is a huge part of this ice cream adventure where our guests are encouraged to "taste the world" through untraditional ice cream varieties and flavours.

Very briefly my ice cream timeline would look something like this:

2001	Ice cream scooping girl, Kerteminde
2008-2012	B.Sc. Food Science, University of Copenhagen
2008-2014	Product developer, Orana A/S Vietnam, Denmark and India
2012 – 2015	M.Sc. Gastronomy and Health, University of Copenhagen
2012	Carpigiani Gelato University, Bologna, Italy (Summer Course)
2014 – 2015	Master thesis, University of Guelph & University of Copenhagen "Functionality of proteins and emulsifiers in ice cream"
2014	Østerberg Ice Cream opens in Copenhagen, Denmark
2015	Guest presenter at the annual "Ice Cream Technology Course", University of Guelph / Professor Douglas Goff
	Awarded the Diploma of Honour, the Danish Gastronomical Academy
2016	Østerberg Ice Cream opens in Ho Chi Minh City, Vietnam
2018	Østerberg Ice Cream expands in Copenhagen
2019	Østerberg Ice Cream school opens in Copenhagen

Starting in the ice cream business has given me so many fantastic experiences, which I never dared to dream as possible. I now also get to work as a consultant for other ice cream companies all over the world, and help them with their recipe developments. I get to teach the science of ice cream through courses on so many levels ranging from young school children to experienced pastry chefs. I get to travel the world, meet amazing and passionate people and work with ice cream. If that is not a dream job, I do not know what is.

Need to know

You might be so excited you just want to head to the kitchen and get started. But if you are going to read only one chapter before making anything in this book, please let it be this one. Then you can always dive into the rest of the book while you are waiting for your ice cream machine to finish. This chapter will help you do certain things in the right way and it will explain the most important aspects of ice cream production.

- Just like everything else in life, balance is essential. In ice cream making the balance between water and solids influences the structure a lot. Hopefully by reading this book you understand why.

- In all the recipes I have made some assumptions about the ingredients. Skimmed milk contains 0% fat. Cream contains 38% fat and the dark chocolate is always 70–80% cocoa solids.

- Egg products are fragile when you heat them because of coagulation and protein denaturation. So if you decide to add egg yolks, egg whites or whole eggs to your base/syrup, please heat it slowly while stirring. If it is heated too fast or not stirred enough you can turn out with "scrambled egg ice cream base". Trust me, this is not something you want. The egg protein science is quite complex, but a rule of thumb is that from around 65°C and above you really need to pay attention and stir frequently.

- After you have heated your base or syrup, you need to let it age for a minimum of 4 hours in the fridge, or preferably overnight. This step is one of the most important ones for building a good ice cream structure. So do not just start 1 hour before you want ice cream...

- Please read the recipes carefully. You might have to adjust some of the base/syrup recipes before adding the flavouring ingredients.

- In general, I believe you are quite clever, so I do not have to point out you need to find bowls, pots and so on. You can see all the equipment you need on page 9.

- If you want to make a good investment, besides this book and an ice cream machine obviously, it should be a set of scales.

- In case your new investment cannot weigh off and detect small amounts such as 2 g of locust bean gum, you can add 1 tsp. I weighed it for you.

- Instead of writing "pour the ice cream mix or sorbet mix in the ice cream machine and freeze until it is scoopable" in the recipes, I write "freeze". It is an ice cream book, and I am pretty sure you would figure that part out. If not, now you know what "freeze" means.

- I might kindly ask you to add the sauce/pieces (if any are added) after the mix has been frozen in the machine. The perfect time is when the ice cream/sorbet is "scoopable" (see definition below).

- I am pretty useless on telling you how long to freeze your mix for in the ice cream machine. This completely depends on your ice cream machine and how much ice cream you are making.

- You can consider your ice cream or sorbet "scoopable" when you can take a spoonful and it is semi-solid and remains on the spoon for at least a few seconds. It should not be so hard that it is not scoopable.

- The boxes called "science notes" make so much more sense, if you have read the theory on ice cream science in the back of this book.

- We want ice crystals in our ice cream and sorbet. But the size is important. Small ice crystals make a smooth texture and is the reason an ice cream is an ice cream: it is frozen. More on ice crystals later on.

Definitions

AGEING An essential step for developing the structure. The base or syrup is left in the fridge after pasteurisation and blending/homogenisation. Keep at 5°C for minimum 4 hours, preferably overnight.

BASE Unfrozen liquid mix of ingredients that will become an ice cream when flavouring ingredients are added and frozen down.

COMPOSITION Fat, sugars, MSNF, emulsifiers and stabilisers are the essential components to define for an ice cream composition.

DENATURATION Proteins unfold and change their structure, so they are better at incorporating air into the ice cream and sorbet.

DEXTROSE A sugar (monosaccharide) with a high FPDF.

EMULSIFIERS A compound that can bind two phases that normally do not like to mix, such as water and fat.

FPDF Stands for Freezing Point Depression Factor. This is a value for how much a specific molecule influences the scoopability of an ice cream or sorbet.

GLUCOSE A sugar (monosaccharide) with a lower FPDF and lower relative sweetness than i.e. dextrose. Exists as both dry and liquid.

HOMOGENISATION This is called "blend thoroughly" in this book. With regards to ice cream, it splits larger fat globules into smaller fat globules.

ICE BATH Fill a bowl or your sink with cold water and ice cubes. This is an ice bath, where you can put a bowl with your base or syrup to cool down.

ICE CRYSTALS Are important. They should just be so small that we cannot detect them in the mouth. They are the solid water state.

LOCUST BEAN GUM A natural stabilizer derived from the plant locust bean. Can be purchased in specialty food or health stores. Adding it is to a certain extent optional, but I strongly recommend it for the sake of structure.

MIX Syrup or base + flavouring ingredients. Still liquid.

MSNF Stands for Milk Solids Non-Fat. Milk proteins and milk sugars are the dominating fraction of this. Milk powder is a rich source of MSNF.

PASTEURISATION Heat treatment is carried out for several reasons with regards to safety and structure.

SCOOPABLE When the ice cream or sorbet is neither too hard nor too soft. Just perfect to scoop and/or incorporate pieces.

SOLIDS Everything that is not water in the base, syrup and mix. Except for solid water, which is defined as ice crystals (nobody said food science was simple).

STABILISERS A group of compounds that increase viscosity and hereby stabilise the structure during storage and temperature fluctuations.

STRUCTURE I wrote an entire thesis on this topic. For now, just know that this is the scientific explanation behind texture.

SUCROSE A sugar (disaccharide) often referred to as table sugar. Used as reference to determine relative sweetness and FPDF.

SUGARS The overall term for sugars such as sucrose, glucose and dextrose.

SYRUP The unfrozen liquid mix of ingredients that will become a sorbet when flavouring ingredients are added and frozen down.

Nice to know

ICE CREAM is defined by its fat percentage in most countries. A minimum level of 10% dairy fat is quite common. However, some countries have lower levels, for instance Denmark where "ice cream" (Danish: *flødeis*) needs to have a minimum of only 5% dairy fat. Ice cream is often shaped into scoops and served at temperatures around -15°C to -18°C. If you need to get a more detailed legal definition, please consult your national food legislation.

GELATO is actually just the Italian word for ice cream or frozen. However, it is often known to be lower in fat, around 3–8%, but consequently higher in sugars to compensate for the lower level of solids. The lower level of fat and higher level of sugar is partly responsible for the softness of gelato, which is also why gelato is not scooped but rather paddled with a spatula into cups or cones. The serving temperature is often a bit warmer, and usually ranges from -10°C to -15°C.

SORBET can be hard to find a definition for, but usually sorbet is considered as a sugar and water solution without dairy products. Some sorbets, however, may contain milk products and/or egg products, so you always need to check with the manufacturer in order to understand this properly.

DANISH ICE CREAM should be defined, and this book is my take on it. Denmark has a long tradition for creating fresh dairy products of very high quality. I want to emphasise this: using fresh milk and cream gives the best flavour (if you ask me). In Denmark, we are also very aware of creating food products close to nature with a lot of fresh fruits, nuts, herbs, and so on to give a strong but natural flavour profile.

The Nordic Cuisine has also gotten a lot of attention the last few years. In this book, you will be presented with some Nordic recipes such as elderflower, sea buckthorn, rhubarb and liquorice. If you are not living in Denmark, I hope you can get your hands on these and taste the result. Otherwise, come visit Denmark!

ICE CREAM MACHINES could be considered a science on its own. Here the focus is on small household machines. You should know, that when you make ice cream in these, the end result will not be as smooth, airy and free of larger ice crystals, as when you use big batch freezers or industrial continuous freezers. The reason for this is especially due to the time it takes to freeze the ice cream. So sorry to tell you this, but the kind of equipment you freeze your ice cream/sorbet on does matter (as a professional ice cream manufacturer who has spent a small fortune on batch freezers, I am actually quite relieved that I have not thrown money out the window)...

For the purpose of creating the most creamy recipes, I have decided to present ice cream recipes with a fat percentage of 10% or higher and I suggest using egg whites for the sorbets. This is beneficial because the recipes will be frozen on small, household machines, and the requirements are quite different compared to recipes that are frozen on professional machines.

If you are looking for recipes to use on a more professional scale, the recipes can be used as a foundation, but I strongly recommend making a few adjustments on both ingredients and composition. It is beyond the scope of this book to cover these adjustments.

BASE & SYRUP

The majority of the recipes in this book are based on ice cream bases and sorbet syrups. The main advantage of working with bases is that it helps you focus.

Developing the recipes of the bases and syrups is where you focus on getting a good structure. The structure of an ice cream or sorbet can be detected sensorically, and this is what we call texture. Dealing with the structure/texture to begin with allows more time and focus on being creative and balancing the flavours afterwards. In this way we can work on both getting a good texture and a well-balanced flavour without too much confusion.

All the recipes are presented as 1 kg batches. In that way it is easier to scale up or down depending on how much you want to produce and how much your ice cream machine can freeze. I will not write how many people the recipe is for, because honestly this is a very private matter. If you want to indulge in one litre all by yourself, please do. Usually, you can expect one scoop of ice cream to be around 100 ml, so you can do the maths from here.

You can easily make a big batch of base, syrup or mix to save for another day. Just freeze it down quiescently after ageing. This means you pour your liquid base or syrup into smaller containers and you put it in a storage freezer – you do not put it into an ice cream machine or scraped-surface freezer of any kind where air is also added. Then you just defrost the base or syrup in the fridge overnight before you need it.

If you wish to create ice creams or sorbets without using egg products, you can leave these out. The result will just be less airy and denser in structure.

Base 1 Cream

This recipe has a strong cream flavour and a rich mouth feel. It is easy to prepare because it only requires 4 basic ingredients you can get in most supermarkets. The recipe is ideal for the more cream-based flavours such as vanilla, caramel, brownie and so on.

120 g	eggs
230 g	skimmed milk
490 g	cream
160 g	sucrose

PREPARATION

Gently whisk the eggs together in a heavy-bottomed pot, so they are homogenous.

Add the rest of the ingredients. Heat up to 75°C under constant, soft stirring and let sit for 5 minutes at this temperature while stirring. Then blend thoroughly.

Make an ice bath and cool down the base to 5°C while stirring gently. Leave the base to age in the fridge.

SCIENCE NOTES

The composition for this recipe is:

20% total fat, 16% sucrose, 12% whole eggs

Whole eggs are added because we want egg yolks to emulsify and the egg whites give additional total solids and some structure. Egg whites contain proteins, which can help incorporate more air into this quite heavy recipe. The lack of skimmed milk powder means we are lacking MSNF, and the egg white proteins can to a certain extent compensate for this.

The MSNF content has not been set as a parameter in this recipe, because the ingredients at hand were selected to be only those 4. If I had decided to add skimmed milk powder, it would have made sense to define a level of MSNF.

Base 2 Milk

The taste experience is fresher than base 1 and the ice cream will not be too heavy with this base. Additionally, the lower fat content (10%) gives a stronger flavour release from the flavouring ingredients since the milk fat does not depress the aroma molecules as much.

It is recommended to add locust bean gum, as it will add viscosity to the base and create a stronger body in the ice cream.

515 g	skimmed milk
265 g	cream
140 g	sucrose
40 g	skimmed milk powder
40 g	egg yolks
2 g	locust bean gum

PREPARATION

Add all ingredients in a heavy-bottomed pot. Heat up to 85°C under constant, soft stirring and blend thoroughly.

Make an ice bath for the base and cool down to 5°C while stirring gently. Leave the base in the fridge to age.

SCIENCE NOTES

The composition for this recipe is:

10% dairy fat, 14% sucrose, 10% MSNF, 4% egg yolks, 0.2% locust bean gum

Locust bean gum is a polysaccharide derived from the locust bean. It works as a stabiliser in the base because it is really good at binding water in the water phase. The water binding capacity is activated by heat treatment, which increases the viscosity, generating a much stronger-bodied ice cream and departing ice crystal growth. The reason for heating this mix to 85°C is to make sure the locust bean gum dissolves and hydrates properly. Other stabilisers can be used, just check which level of dosage is recommended and the heating temperatures.

Base 3 Sugar specific

Use this recipe if you wish to make ice creams with specific functionalities; less sweet for savoury flavour or sweeter if you have a very sweet tooth; more soft if you are impatient when the ice cream comes out of the -18°C freezer or harder if you wish to add alcohol or make sticks/sandwiches/cakes.

You can easily adjust the different kinds of sugars according to the recommendations given below or in the recipes.

440 g	skimmed milk
315 g	cream
65 g	skimmed milk powder
140 g	sugar *(see suggestions)*
40 g	egg yolks
2 g	locust bean gum

PREPARATION Add all ingredients in a heavy-bottomed pot. Heat up to 85°C under constant, soft stirring and blend thoroughly.

Make an ice bath for the base and cool down to 5°C while stirring gently. Leave the base in the fridge to age.

SCIENCE NOTES

The composition for this recipe is:

12% dairy fat, 14% sugar, 12% MSNF, 4% egg yolks, 0.2% locust bean gum

Of course the option of adding more or less sugar is also present. But keep in mind that we need to have a certain balance and amount of total solids in the ice cream, and in general consuming too much sugar is not ideal for anything.

I suggest you to keep minimum 60–80 g sucrose/kg mix in the recipe to make sure it has a certain level of sweetness and softness regardless of the other kinds of sugar you decide to use.

Read more on page 135 to find out how the different types of sugar affects ice creams and sorbets.

VARIATIONS

Recommendations for specific ice cream functionalities based on sugar varieties:

A. SOFTER	60 g sucrose + 80 g dextrose
B. LESS SWEET AND HARDER	60 g sucrose + 80 g glucose
C. STANDARD	100 g sucrose + 40 g glucose

VARIETY A will be used for flavours that include more fatty ingredients, such as nuts and chocolate. The extra fat makes the ice cream harder and hence dextrose is needed to make it softer.

VARIETY B is ideal for ice cream sticks, cookies and ice creams containing alcohol. For these it is beneficial to work with a base that is harder.

VARIETY C is simply another version of an ice cream base, where the level of sweetness is a bit lower than if just sucrose is used.

Syrup 1 Simple

This recipe is the simplest to make, but does not always give best the structure. So, if you need to mix up a sorbet fast and easy and eat it right away, I can definitely recommend this recipe.

500 g	sucrose
450 g	water
50 g	egg whites

PREPARATION Add all ingredients in a heavy-bottomed pot. Heat up to 75°C under constant, soft stirring and leave at this temperature for 5 minutes. Then blend thoroughly.

Cool down in an ice bath until it reaches 5°C while stirring and then leave in the fridge to age.

SCIENCE NOTES

The composition for this recipe is:

Syrup: 50% sucrose, 5% egg whites

Sorbet: 50% fruit, 25% sucrose, 2.5% egg whites

This syrup is best suited for recipes containing whole fruits or berries due to a higher level of dietary fibres. I do not recommend storing sorbets made with this syrup for a long time in the freezer since the structure is very fragile. This means it can separate out, it will not have as much air to help stabilise the structure and the ice crystals can grow quite large. So, this sorbet should be consumed immediately.

If you were going to skip the ageing step in one recipe in this book, it should be this one. The only reason we want to age this syrup is for the proteins to hydrate completely and for it to cool down before working with it.

Syrup 2 Stronger structure

This recipe has a stronger structure than syrup 1 because we are adding locust bean gum and glucose. Both play a key role in increasing viscosity of the sorbet syrup.

500 g	water
300 g	sucrose
150 g	glucose
5 g	locust bean gum
50 g	egg white

PREPARATION Add all ingredients in a heavy-bottomed pot. Heat up to 85°C under constant, soft stirring and blend thoroughly.

Cool down in an ice bath until it reaches 5°C under constant, slow stirring. Leave in the fridge to age.

SCIENCE NOTES

The composition for this recipe is:

Syrup: 30% sucrose, 15% glucose, 0.5% locust bean gum, 5% egg white.

Sorbet: 50% fruit, 15% sucrose, 7.5% glucose, 0.25% locust bean gum, 2.5% egg whites

As can be seen in table 3 on page 135, glucose has a lower level of sweetness than sucrose and a lower freezing point depression factor (FPDF), meaning the sorbet will be less sweet and soft as for instance syrup 1.

I recommend ageing this syrup in order to dissolve and hydrate the locust bean gum and egg whites properly so it will help create the most viscous texture it can.

SIDE NOTE

In a few of the recipes, I recommend you add only 20–30 g egg whites per kg of syrup. These are the recipes that contain ingredients with a high level of acidity such as elderflower, grapefruit and kombucha. Acid increases the protein denaturation, which helps with incorporating air. So if the amount of egg whites is not adjusted, we end up with a sorbet that has a mousse-like texture due to high air incorporation.

WEIGHT

Showing weight of the different scoops of ice creams and sorbets. It can be seen that the scoops with egg yolks and egg whites are lighter because more air has been incorporated.

Ice cream without egg yolks — 35 g

Ice cream with egg yolks — 29 g

Sorbet without egg whites — 36 g

Sorbet with egg whites — 32 g

Syrup 3 Sugar specific

Similarly to the ice cream base 3, this is the recipe where we can play around with the different kinds of sugar and make the sorbet softer, harder, sweeter or less sweet.

450 g	water
500 g	sugars *(see suggestions below)*
5 g	locust bean gum
50 g	egg white

PREPARATION Add all ingredients in a heavy-bottomed pot. Heat up to 85°C under constant, soft stirring and blend thoroughly. Cool down in an ice bath until it reaches 5°C while stirring and then leave in the fridge to age.

SCIENCE NOTES

The composition for this recipe is:

Syrup: 50% sugars, 0.5% locust bean gum, 5% egg white

Sorbet: 50% fruit, 25% sugars, 0.25% locust bean gum, 2.5% egg whites

VARIATIONS Recommendations for specific functionalities based on sugar varieties:

A. ALTERNATIVE SWEETENER	500 g honey/syrup*
B. LESS SWEET AND HARDER	300 g glucose + 200 g sucrose
C. STANDARD	300 g sucrose + 150 g glucose + 50 g dextrose

VARIETY A is used when you wish to sweeten with different sweeteners.

VARIETY B is ideal for making sorbets containing alcohol, since alcohol depresses the freezing point and makes it softer. This syrup is harder than C.

VARIETY C is how you could make a sorbet in order to get a good balance between being soft and sweet.

---

* There is water present in honey and syrups. Either you neglect this and accept there will be less sugar and lower sweetness, or you can account for that by adding more, so you get 500 g sugars (look at the nutritional content and calculate how much honey/syrup you need to add in order to get 500 g sugar) and remove that excess water from the water content in the recipe.

RECIPES

Now that we know how to produce ice cream bases and sorbet syrups, we will move on to the step that requires more emphasis on good taste buds and creativeness and less scientific skills: adding the wonderful and tasty ingredients.

A good bit of advice is to taste the recipes before you freeze them in the ice cream machine (I know, it is a hard job, but someone has to do it...). Your taste buds are different from mine, and we might not use identical ingredients so it is good to get a sense of what you enjoy. As long as the mix is still liquid you can change it. Once frozen, you cannot redo it! So just bear in mind you want the mix to be a little bit sweeter than the frozen product. The perception of sweetness changes with temperature.

I recommend one specific base or syrup for each recipe, but feel free to use one of the other bases or syrups if you prefer.

A small piece of advice to start with is making sure that everything is as cold as possible. So turn on your ice cream machine 15–20 minutes before you are ready to start freezing. Many ice cream machines have a small bowl, which you pour the ice cream mix in and place in the "machine bowl". If your machine has this inserted bowl, put the bowl in the freezer first, so that it is as cold as possible, too. If you have this bowl, pour some ethanol into the "machine bowl" and make sure it goes up on the sides; alcohol conducts the cold really well. Just promise me you will not get the ethanol in the mix since it will change the sensorical experience quite drastically – and not for the better...

I recommend enjoying the ice cream straight from the ice cream machine. If you put it in a storage freezer, it will get harder and consequently a bit icier (more of the water phase goes into the solid state, creating ice crystals that, with a high probability, will become big enough to detect in the mouth). If you do put it in the freezer, I recommend taking it out 10-15 minutes before serving to make sure the serving temperature is -12 to -15°C.

In the last chapter of this book, I have written a small paragraph on the shelf-life of ice creams and storage.

On page 47 and 88 I am showing you recipes that are ideal if you wish to add 25% of a liquid ingredient or up to 30% fruit to an ice cream respectively. If you add this high amount without compensating in the base, it will get very icy, hard and cold in the mouth because of the extra water content from the liquid/fruit.

The recipes are not presented alphabetically, so I recommend you look at the index in order to find what you are looking for. The design and aesthetics of the book matter a bit more than putting them alphabetically.

Buttermilk, vanilla & lemon

These three ingredients are the foundation of making a very famous Danish snack/dessert called "koldskål" ("cold bowl" translated directly). We usually eat it in summer time with broken up "kammerjunker" (a special kind of cookie) on top. Feel free to add the cookies after it has been frozen.

This recipe is composed like a sorbet, but it contains buttermilk, which contributes with some MSNF and milk fat, and that helps generate a bit of structure.

500 g	sorbet syrup 3, variety C
480 g	buttermilk
20 g	lime juice
1	vanilla pod

PREPARATION Scrape out the seeds from the vanilla pod and blend all the ingredients together and freeze.

Turn to page 51 for recommendation on working with vanilla.

Chocolate sorbet

Chocolate sorbet combines the best from two worlds: the intense flavour that comes from a sorbet and the creamy, rich texture that ice cream can bring. This is possible because chocolate and cocoa solids contains fat, proteins and fibre, which all help generate a strong texture. If you want the recipe to be a bit more airy, add 4% egg yolks (40 g in the below recipe) in order to emulsify the fat in the water phase and hence stabilise the air bubbles a little better.

600 g	water
60 g	cacao powder *(22–24% fat content)*
190 g	sucrose
40 g	dextrose
2 g	locust bean gum
100 g	dark chocolate

PREPARATION Mix water, cacao powder, sucrose, dextrose and locust bean gum in a heavy-bottomed pot under constant stirring. Heat it up to 85°C and blend it thoroughly. Cool the mix down to 60–65°C and blend in the chocolate until homogenous. Leave the mix in the fridge to age.

Give the mix a little stir before you put it in the ice cream machine and freeze.

SCIENCE NOTES

The composition for this recipe is:

6% fat, 22% sucrose, 4% dextrose, 8% other solids

In order to do the calculations for this recipe, we need to do some maths (I left it out for you to try yourself). We have two sources of fat (cocoa and chocolate), two sources of sucrose (pure sucrose and the sucrose present in the chocolate) and two sources of other solids (cacao and chocolate). Other solids here are mainly composed of fibres and proteins.

The total sugar content is similar to that of sorbets despite the fat and other solids content. This is partly due to the fact that cocoa and chocolate generates some bitter flavours that need to be balanced. Tasting it, you probably will not feel this to be sweeter than a regular ice cream.

Chocolate ice cream

One of the most popular flavours in the ice cream shops: chocolate. Chocolate ice cream can either be super intense or milder and more elegant. I prefer to go for mild and elegant and refer to the chocolate sorbet if you wish to enjoy a very rich chocolate scoop.

I like having pieces in my chocolate ice cream, so I have suggested that below.

900 g	base 3, variety A
100 g	chocolate
75 g	chocolate

PREPARATION Heat the base with the 100 g chocolate until it is dissolved. Blend until there are no small pieces of chocolate left. Cool down in an ice bath until the mix is 5°C and freeze. Somewhere in the "waiting time", chop the chocolate. Once scoopable, add the chopped chocolate pieces.

Cinnamon & white chocolate

Personally, I think cinnamon should be enjoyed all year around, so make this recipe anytime you wish. If you think it belongs to Christmas time, please make it around Christmas time and help underline the fact that ice cream for sure can be enjoyed all year around.

1000 g	base 1
10 g	ground cinnamon
100 g	caramelized white chocolate *(see below)*

PREPARATION Blend the base and cinnamon together and chop the white chocolate. Freeze and once it is scoopable, gently fold in the white chocolate.

Matcha & white chocolate

Matcha is for many people an acquired taste. Personally, I love it! Matcha is a Japanese green tea, where the specially grown green tea leaves are powdered and consumed (not just an extract like regular green tea). The flavour is dry, green, grassy and a little bitter. The best comment I have received after serving it in the ice cream shops: "It tastes like fish!" Well… I think we eat very different types of fish dear customer!

1000 g	base 1
10 g	matcha powder
100 g	caramelized white chocolate *(see below)*

PREPARATION Blend the base and matcha together and chop the white chocolate. Freeze and once it is scoopable, gently fold in the white chocolate.

CARAMELISED WHITE CHOCOLATE Preheat the oven at 140°C convection. Spread out 200 g white chocolate on a baking tray and then put it in the oven for 10–12 minutes or until it is golden (you know your oven better than me – so please keep an eye out for this to make sure it does not burn). Leave it to cool and chop it up. It can be stored in an airtight container for several weeks.

Cucumber, mint & lime sorbet

This recipe is extremely suitable for mixing together with your gin & tonic on a Friday night. Besides making the G&T so much tastier, it also saves you the ice cubes.

500 g	sorbet syrup 3, variety C
430 g	cucumber
70 g	lime juice
1 handful	mint leaves

PREPARATION Chop the cucumber into 1x1 (ish) cm pieces. Add the glucose to the cucumber and let it sit for 20 minutes. Add half of the sorbet syrup and blend together first (when you have less liquid it is easier to blend out the cucumber). Once blended thoroughly, add the mint leaves and blend some more. The more you blend it, the smoother your sorbet will be.

Add the rest of the sorbet syrup, and lime juice and blend a little more before freezing.

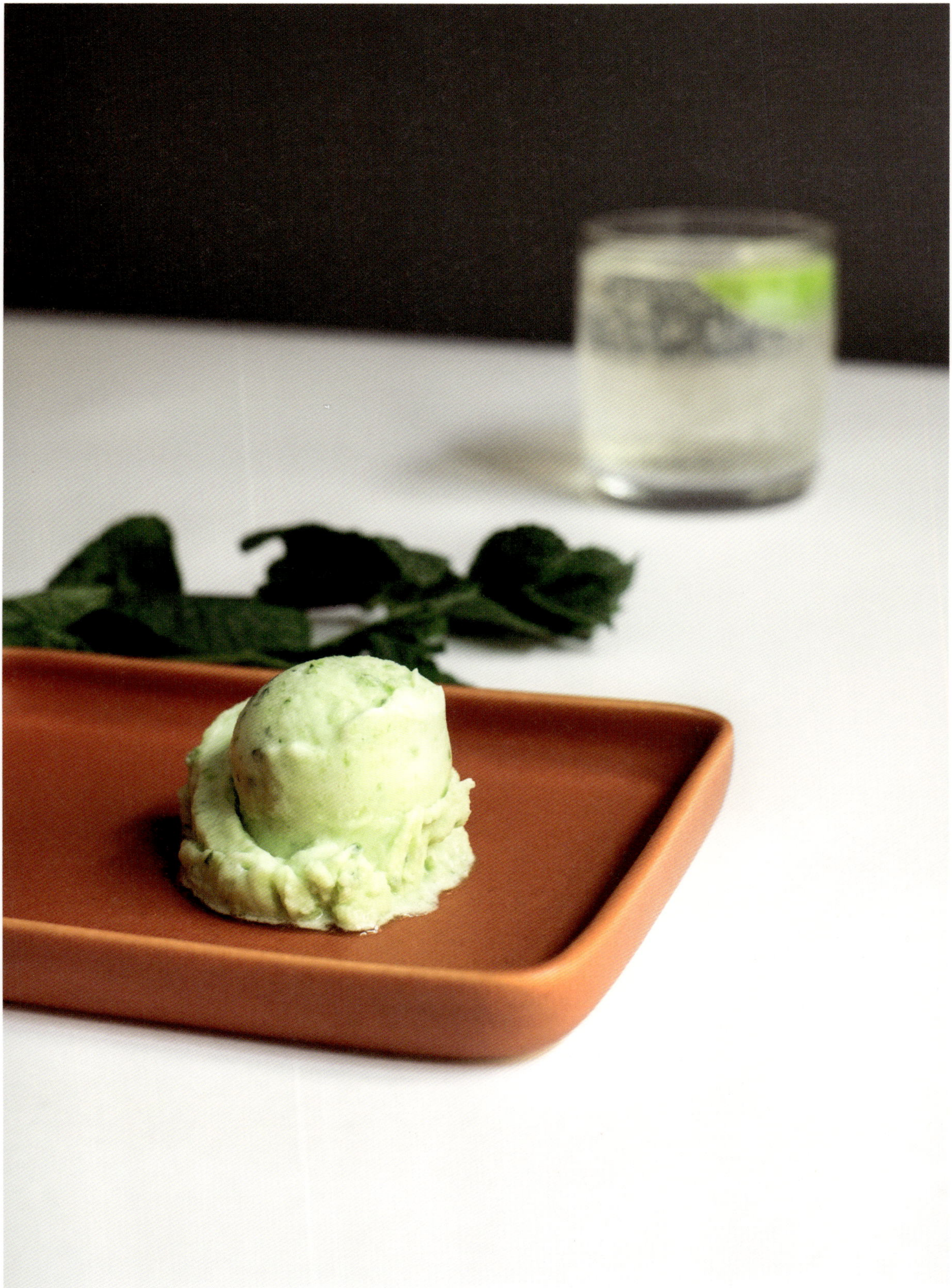

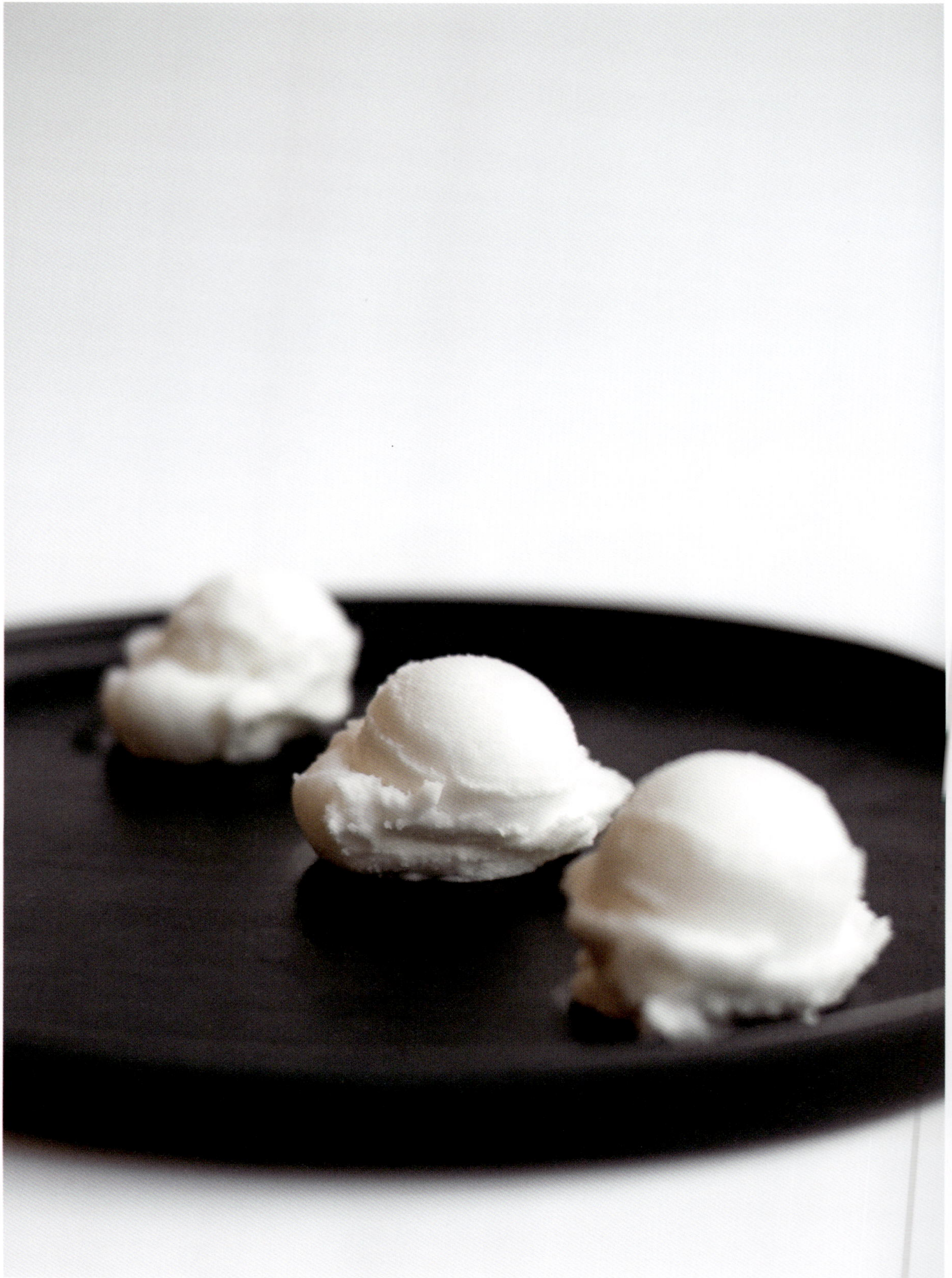

Gin & yuzu sorbet

Yuzu is a Japanese citrus fruit, which has a very aromatic flavour. Scoop this sorbet up in a cocktail glass and serve with a drizzle of estragon on top, it is the perfect cocktail for any occasion. Period.

500 g	syrup 3, variety B
225 g	yuzu juice
175 g	water
100 g	gin

PREPARATION — Mix all the ingredients together and freeze.

Mangosteen sorbet

Mangosteen is quite common to find in Asia, so when I was living in Vietnam working on opening Østerberg Ice Cream parlour, I enjoyed a lot of native fruits, hereunder mangosteen. It has a delicate, sweet flavour – almost like a melon, just better.

Getting your hands on this exotic fruit requires a good fruit supplier but it is getting more and more available.

500 g	syrup 2
500 g	mangosteen pulp
10 g	lemon juice

PREPARATION — Blend all the ingredients together and freeze.

Avocado & lime sorbet with dates

I quite often get asked how I come up with the different flavour combinations. My reply: they can come from everywhere from going to the supermarket looking at ingredients to friends and customers suggesting new combinations. This particular recipe actually came from my choice of snacks; often I cut up an avocado and put a date where the pit was and drizzle a bit of lime juice on it; the sweet and chewy date combined with a rich avocado with notes of citrus is one of my daily pleasures.

500 g	sorbet syrup
400 g	avocado pulp
75 g	lime juice
25 g	water
75 g	medjoul dates

PREPARATION

The syrup, avocado, lime and water is blended together and frozen.

Chop the dates into small pieces.

When the sorbet is frozen until scoopable, the date pieces are gently mixed into the sorbet.

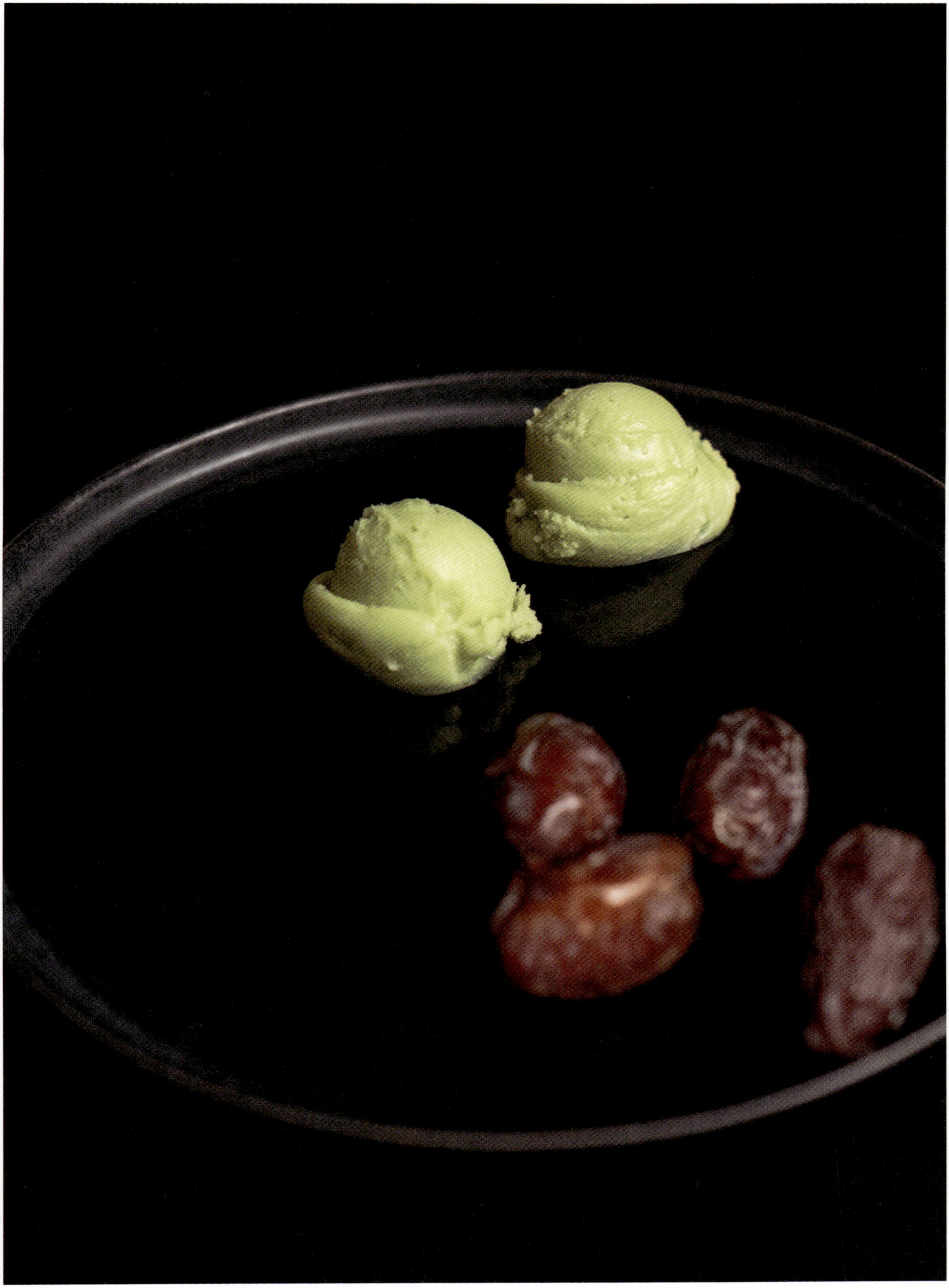

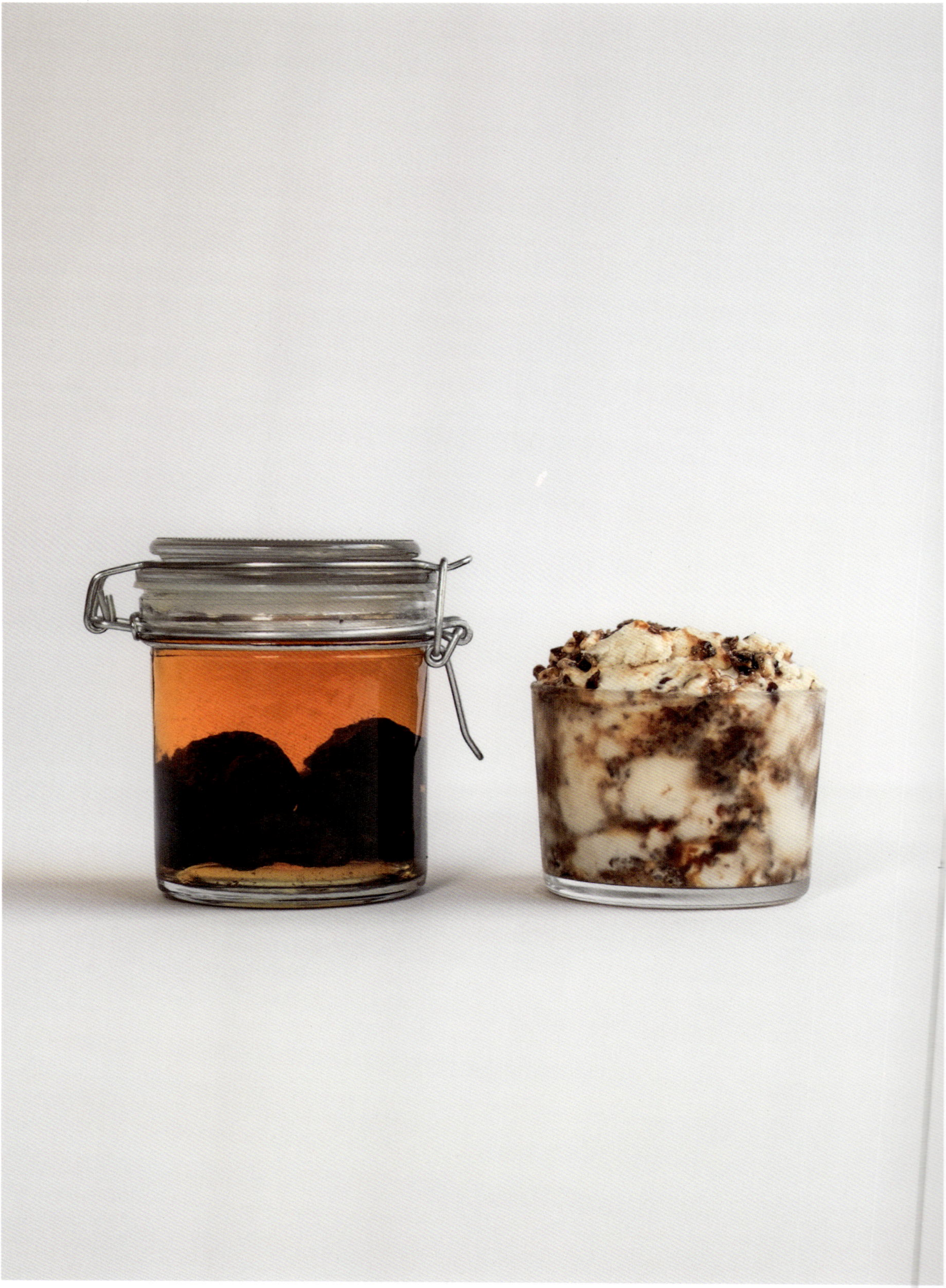

Drunk prunes

This recipe could also be called prunes in Armagnac. Ideal for desserts when you want to add a bit more of a punch and intensify your usual scoop of vanilla ice cream on the side.

1000 g	base 2
75 g	prunes
75 g	Armagnac

PREPARATION Put the prunes in a small bowl and cover with Armagnac. Leave them to sit at least overnight, preferably days in advance.

Blend the prune/Armagnac mix until there are no whole prunes, but there is still texture left in the prunes. Add 50 g of the mix to the ice cream base, and freeze. Once it is scoopable, fold in the remaining prunes/Armagnac and enjoy.

Elderflower sorbet

Creating an intense sorbet out of elderflowers can be tricky if you cannot get your hands on an extract without a lot of sugar. I have created this recipe using a cordial, which contains around 40–50% sugar. Because the sugar content is so high, none of the sorbet syrups provided in this book are ideal for this, and we need to recalculate a recipe based on the cordial with 40–50% sugar. A lot of Danes choose to make their own elderflower cordial. If you do, aim for a similar sugar content, an intense elderflower flavour and follow the recipe below.

530 g	elderflower cordial
450 g	water
20 g	egg whites
3 g	locust bean gum

PREPARATION Heat water, locust bean gum and egg whites in a heavy-bottomed pot under constant stirring until it reaches 85°C. Cool down in an ice bath until it reaches 5°C while stirring gently. Add the elderflower cordial and leave it in the fridge to age. Then freeze.

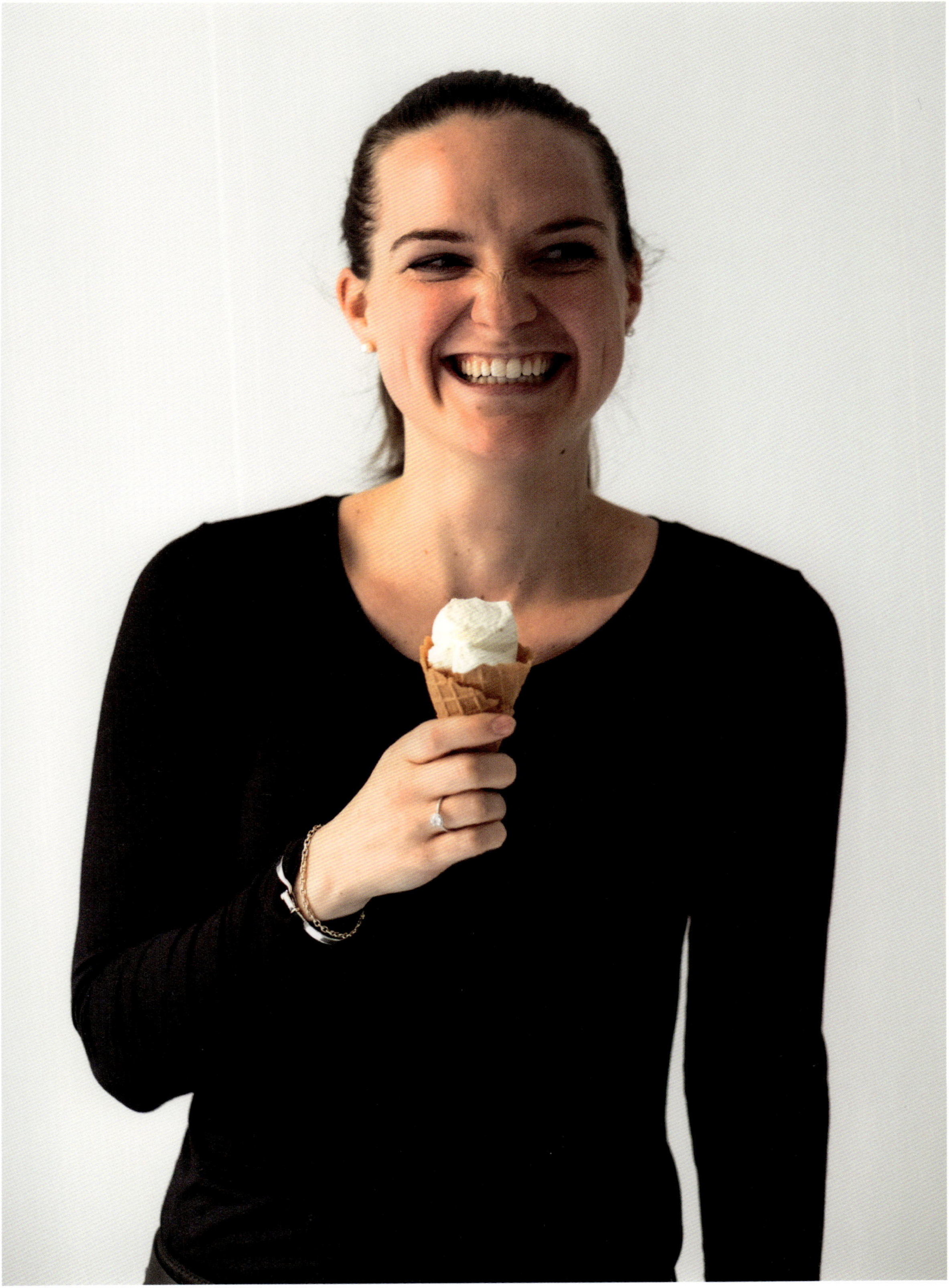

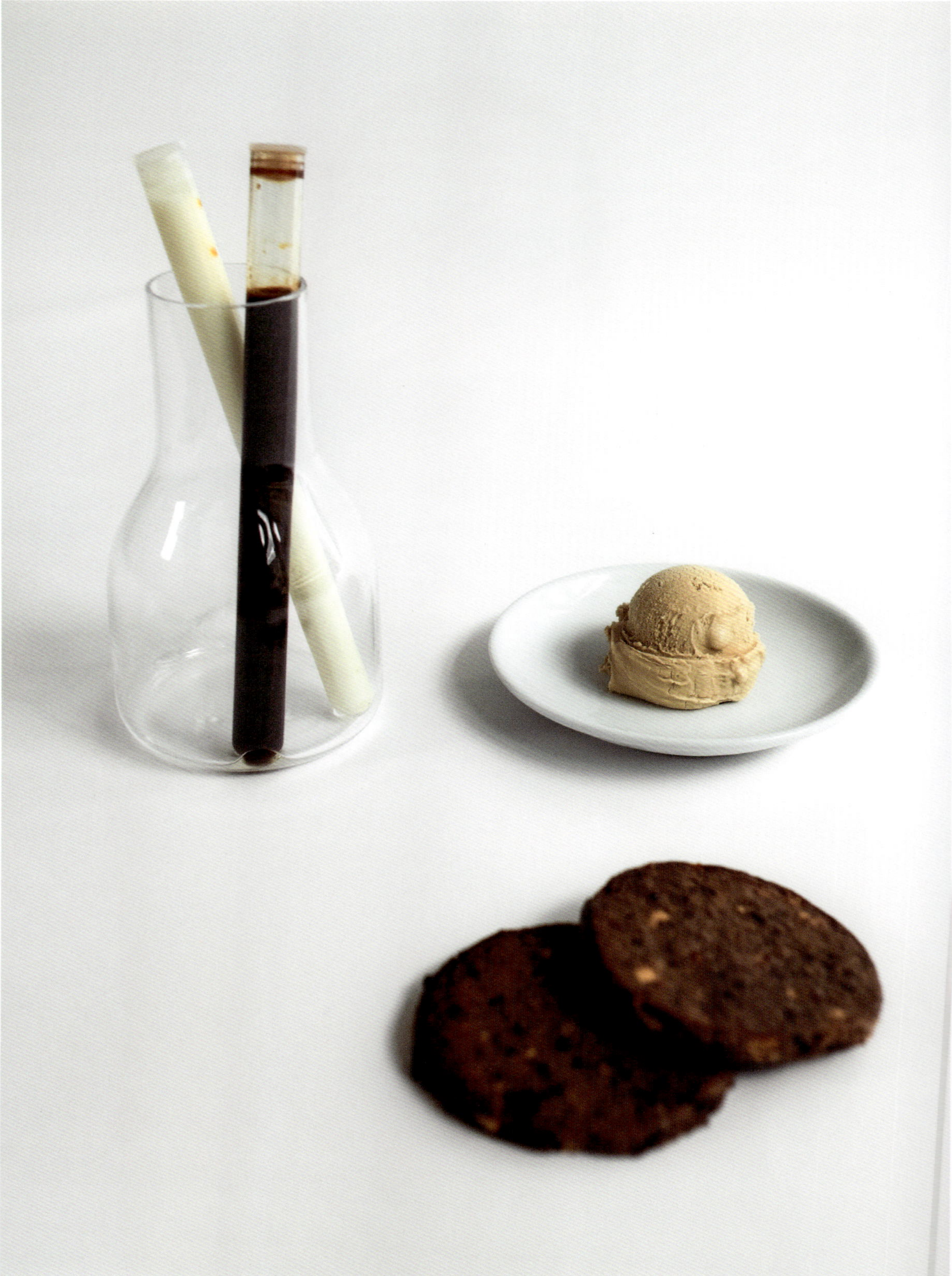

Espresso ice cream

An intense espresso flavour combined with a rich ice cream. What is not to like?

265 g	cream
215 g	skimmed milk
120 g	sucrose
70 g	skimmed milk powder
40 g	glucose
40 g	egg yolk
2 g	locust bean gum
250 g	espresso

PREPARATION

Add all the ingredients except for espresso in a heavy-bottomed pot and heat up until it reaches 85°C under constant stirring. Blend it really well, put in an ice bath to cool down to 5°C and leave to age. This recipe will be quite thick since 25% liquid is missing.

Blend the base together with the espresso and freeze.

Adding around 10% whiskey to this recipe is not the worst idea someone could get. And adding some caramelized white chocolate from page 35... Yes please!

SCIENCE NOTES

The composition for this recipe is:

25% espresso, 16% total sugars, 10% dairy fat, 10% MSNF, 4% egg yolks, 0.2% locust bean gum

The attentive reader might have noticed that this recipe is identical to the one for beer. This can help you if you want to create an ice cream where you similarly have to add a liquid and want an intense flavoured ice cream. Because if you just add a lot of liquid to one of the bases, the ice cream will become very icy, flaky and cold in the mouth because the base is no longer balanced with regards to the water and solid ratio.

Beer ice cream with peanut nougat

Beer and peanuts: the perfect combination. There is something so odd and unusual about a beer ice cream, which makes it interesting. It can be really hard to find the right audience. Having served this in our ice cream parlours, I noticed a pattern: women in general tended to like an ice cream which did not taste like beer while men just wanted their beer without dairy products. Nevertheless, a few people (myself included) still appreciate this balance between sweet and bitter. Personally, I like to use a dark Porter to add some caramel notes to the ice cream.

265 g	cream
215 g	skimmed milk
120 g	sucrose
70 g	skimmed milk powder
40 g	glucose
40 g	egg yolk
2 g	locust bean gum
250 g	beer
100 g	peanut nougat *(see page 97 for recipe)*

PREPARATION

Add all the ingredients, except for beer and nougat, in a heavy-bottomed pot and heat up until it reaches 85°C whilst constantly stirring. Blend it really well and leave to age in the fridge. Do not be surprised when you see how thick this base is. It lacks 25% liquid.

Blend the base together with the beer and freeze. When the ice cream is scoopable, add the chopped nougat pieces and serve it for your next happy hour (or soccer game).

SCIENCE NOTES

The composition for this recipe is:

25% beer, 16% total sugars, 10% dairy fat, 10% MSNF, 4% egg yolks, 0.2% locust bean gum

We do not want to heat up the beer, because the alcohol will evaporate, and that is a shame! The alcohol in the finished ice cream will result in an ice cream that is a bit softer than most other ice creams due to the FPDF seen in table 3 on page 135. However, this just makes it easier to eat straight out of the freezer.

You can add sucrose instead of glucose if you prefer.

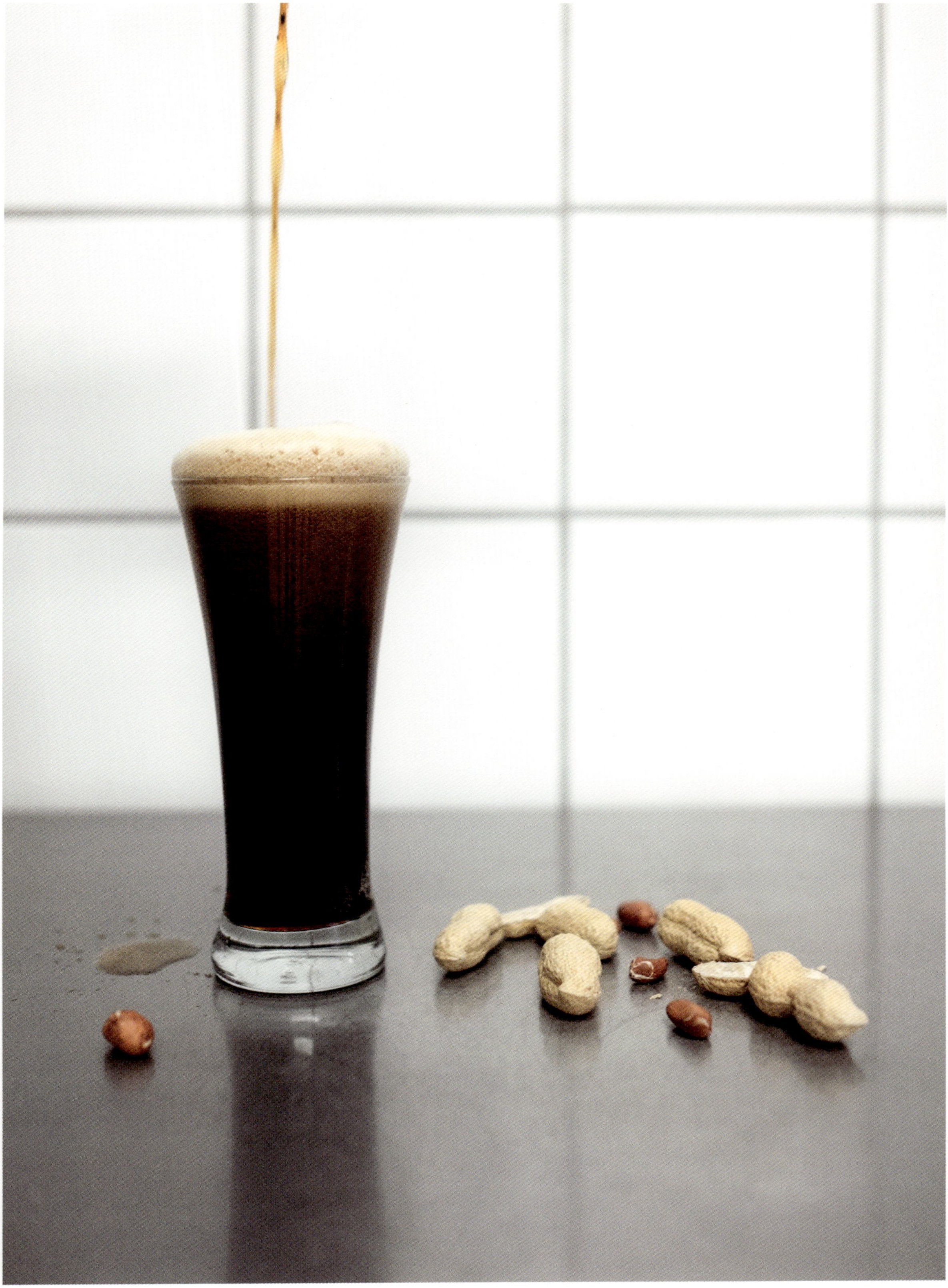

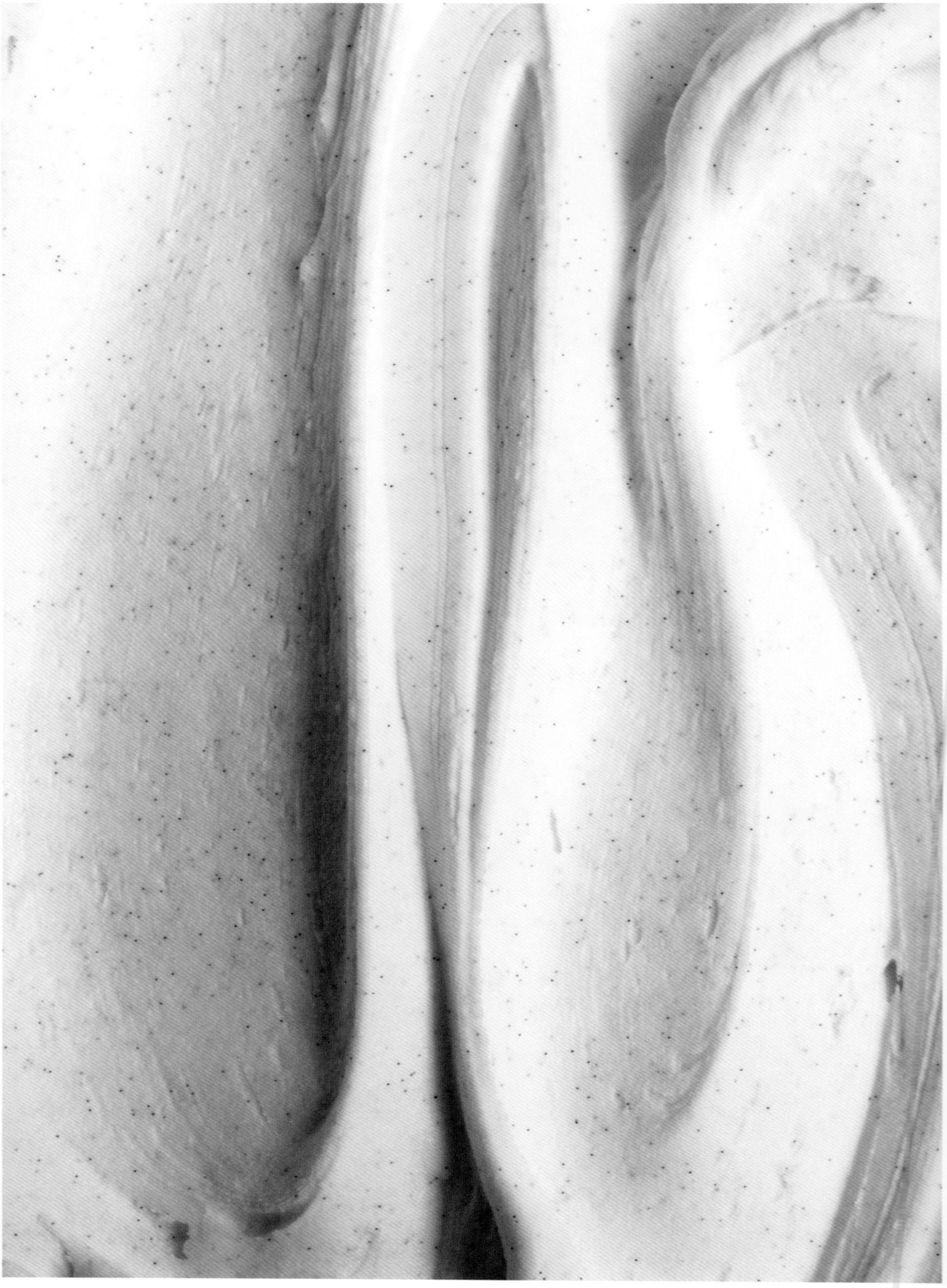

Vanilla

Something as simple as vanilla can actually be the hardest one to get right. Especially with the vanilla prices increasing like they have been the past many years. Nevertheless, buy the best vanilla you can find, because only the best ingredients are good enough for this ice cream. My rule of thumb when visiting ice cream parlours and restaurants: if you cannot see small black vanilla specs, it is not "real vanilla" to me. I want to see the seeds from inside the pod.

I often see people coming into our shops for the first time and ask to try the vanilla. This is sort of the reference point for many. The general belief is, if you know how to make a good vanilla, you know how to make good ice cream.

1000 g	base of your choice
2	vanilla pods
1 pinch	sea salt

PREPARATION Scrape the beans out of the vanilla pods (save the pods) and add the beans to the base together with the sea salt. Blend and freeze.

WORKING WITH VANILLA There are many types of vanilla grown in different areas with varying flavour and quality. To select your preferred vanilla, you might have to taste your way through the different varieties.

Personally, I really like a mix of Polynesian (also called Tahitian vanilla) and Bourbon vanilla. Bourbon vanilla has a cleaner vanilla flavour, is usually cheaper, and the pods are quite thin. Polynesian vanilla has a more flowery/spicy flavour profile, it is thicker and is usually quite expensive. So, a mixture is ideal.

With vanilla prices being very high, I strongly recommend you scrape the pod really well and keep the empty pods in a jar with some sugar to create your own vanilla sugar. You can also put the entire pod in with the base as the base is heated to get as much vanilla flavour out as possible.

Is-à-la-mande

This is my ice cream take on a very special Danish Christmas dessert called ris-à-la-mande (rice with almonds). In Denmark, we eat it for dessert Christmas Eve, but personally I like this so much that I can eat it all year round.

1000 g	base 1
2	vanilla pods
50 g	skinless almonds
50 g	cherry sauce

PREPARATION Prepare the cherry sauce from page 107 and chop the almonds.

Scrape the seeds out of the vanilla pods and blend it into the base. Turn to page 51 for working with vanilla.

Freeze the vanilla ice cream. When it is scoopable, you gently fold in the almond flakes and cherry sauce. Værsgo (bon appetite in Danish).

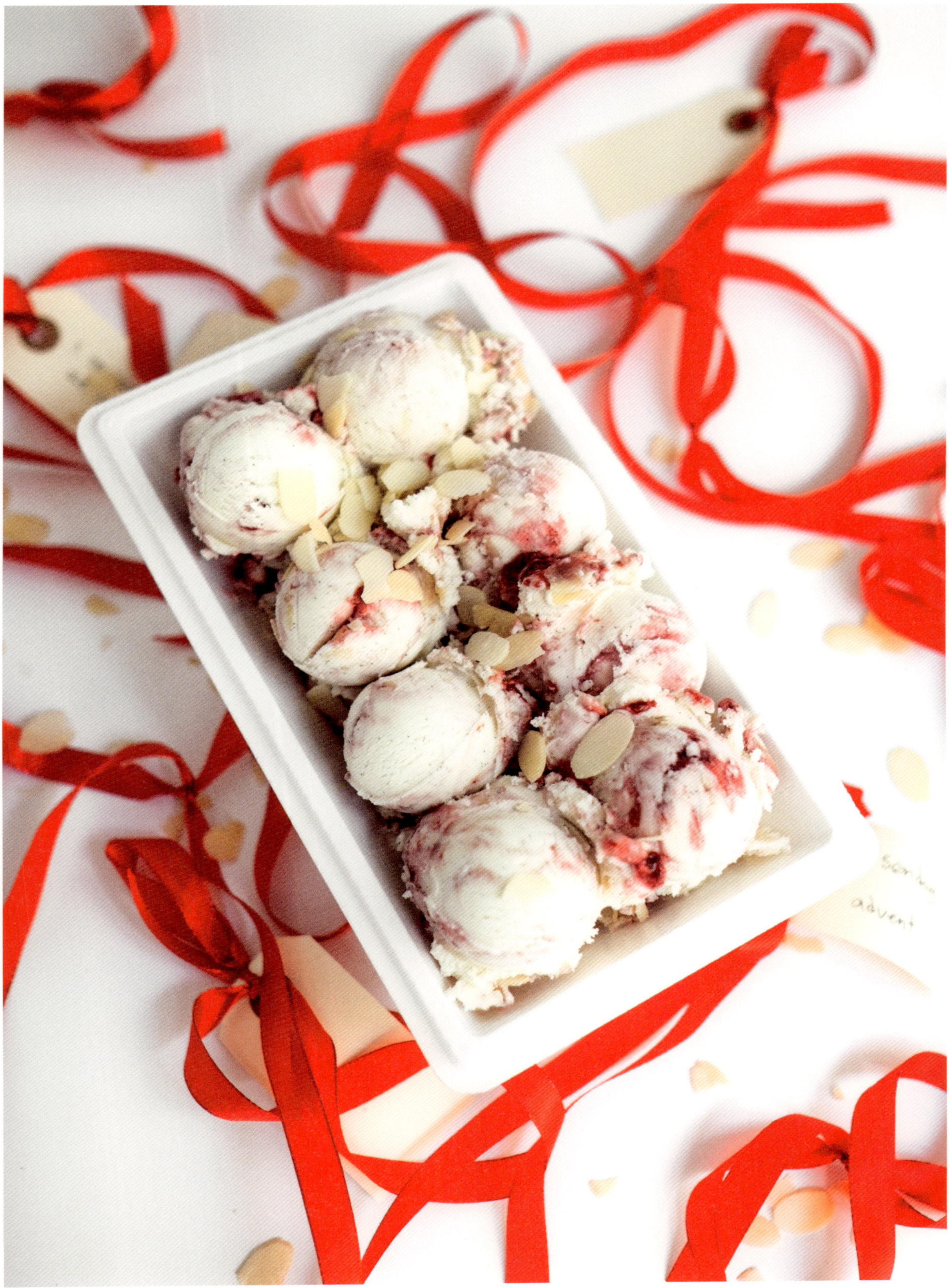

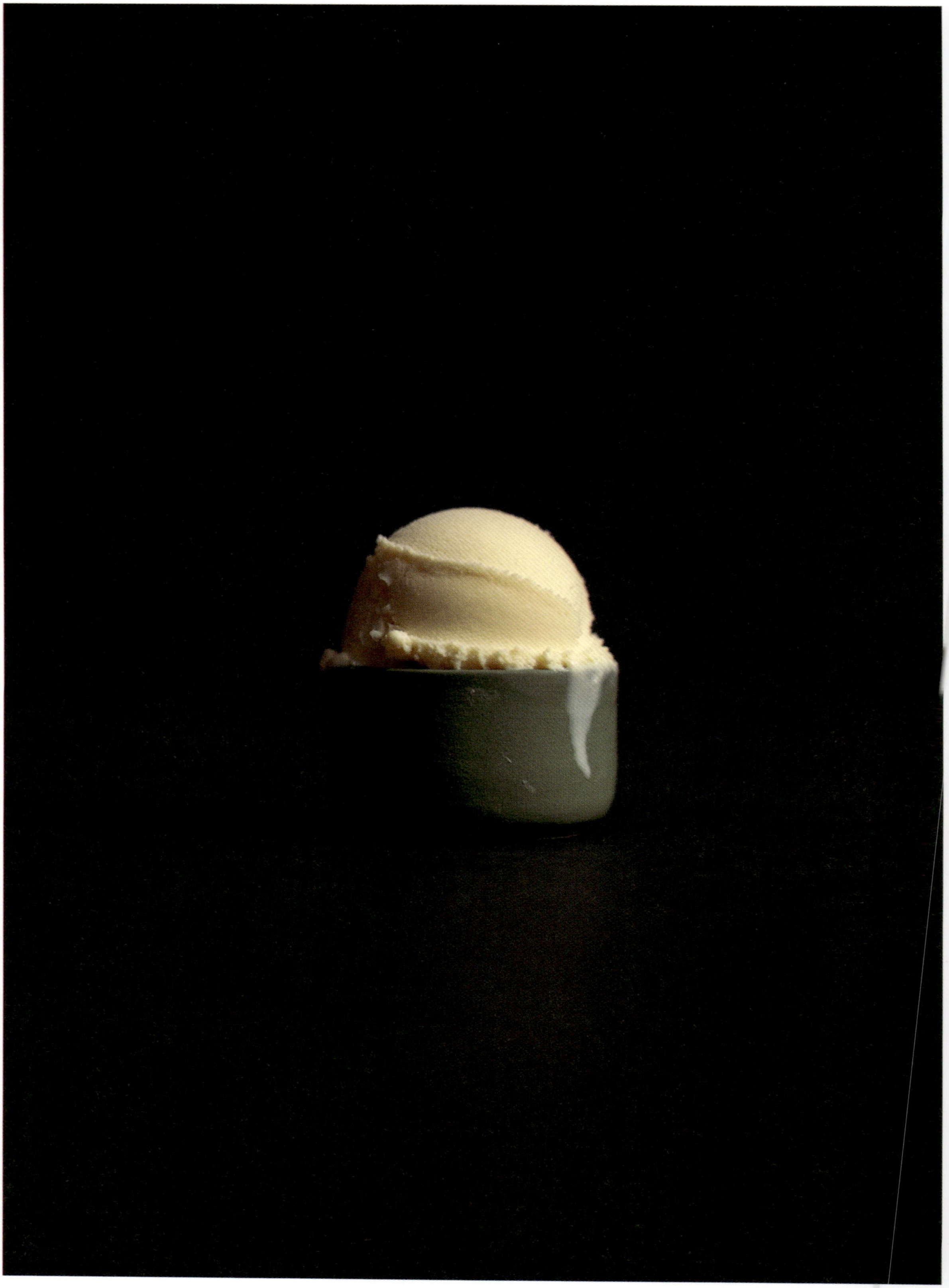

Jackfruit ice cream

Getting your hands on a jackfruit might be the hardest part, but visiting specialty stores increases your chances of finding it. The flavour profile of jackfruit is best described as a mango/banana/pineapple mixture.

PREPARATION

Now turn to page 47 and replace espresso with jackfruit. Voila.

You can either choose to use the jackfruit fresh and accept some small bits and pieces in your ice cream or boil the jackfruit until it is tender and then the flavour tastes a little more cooked.

Make the base the day before and then blend the jackfruit in and freeze the mix.

If you want to try this as a sorbet, you simply take 50% jackfruit and 50% sorbet syrup 2.

Passionfruit & Earl Grey

The sharp acidic notes from passion fruit go very well with the rounder and almost bitter notes from Earl Grey tea. I developed this recipe in Vietnam after a customer suggested it.

500 g	sorbet syrup 2 *(note: only add 20 g egg white / kg syrup)*
250 g	passion fruit juice
250 g	water
1 tbsp	Earl Grey tea leaves

PREPARATION

Be aware that the syrup is adjusted from the syrup presented on page 23. We need less egg whites due to the high acidity.

Boil the water and pour it onto the tea leaves. Leave to sit for 7–8 minutes and then blend together with the passionfruit juice and sorbet syrup. Strain away the tea leaves and freeze.

Lavender nougat

Lavender is a very aromatic flower, which goes through very well in an ice cream. I like to add a bit of caramelised lavender crunch to it, just to add some more complex flavours to the very clean lavender flavour.

1000 g	base 2
6 g	dried lavender flowers
100 g	lavender nougat *(see page 97 for recipe)*

PREPARATION Add the 6 g of dried lavender flowers to the ice cream base and blend really well. Heat the mix up for 5 minutes at 50–60°C.

While the base is heating, start making the nougat.

When the base has been heated, taste it. If you find that it needs more lavender flavour for your preference, blend it again and let it sit for another 10 minutes. If you still want more flavour, please add another 3 g of lavender flowers, blend and let it sit for another 5–10 minutes. Then strain away the lavenders and freeze.

When the ice cream is scoopable, fold in the chopped lavender nougat.

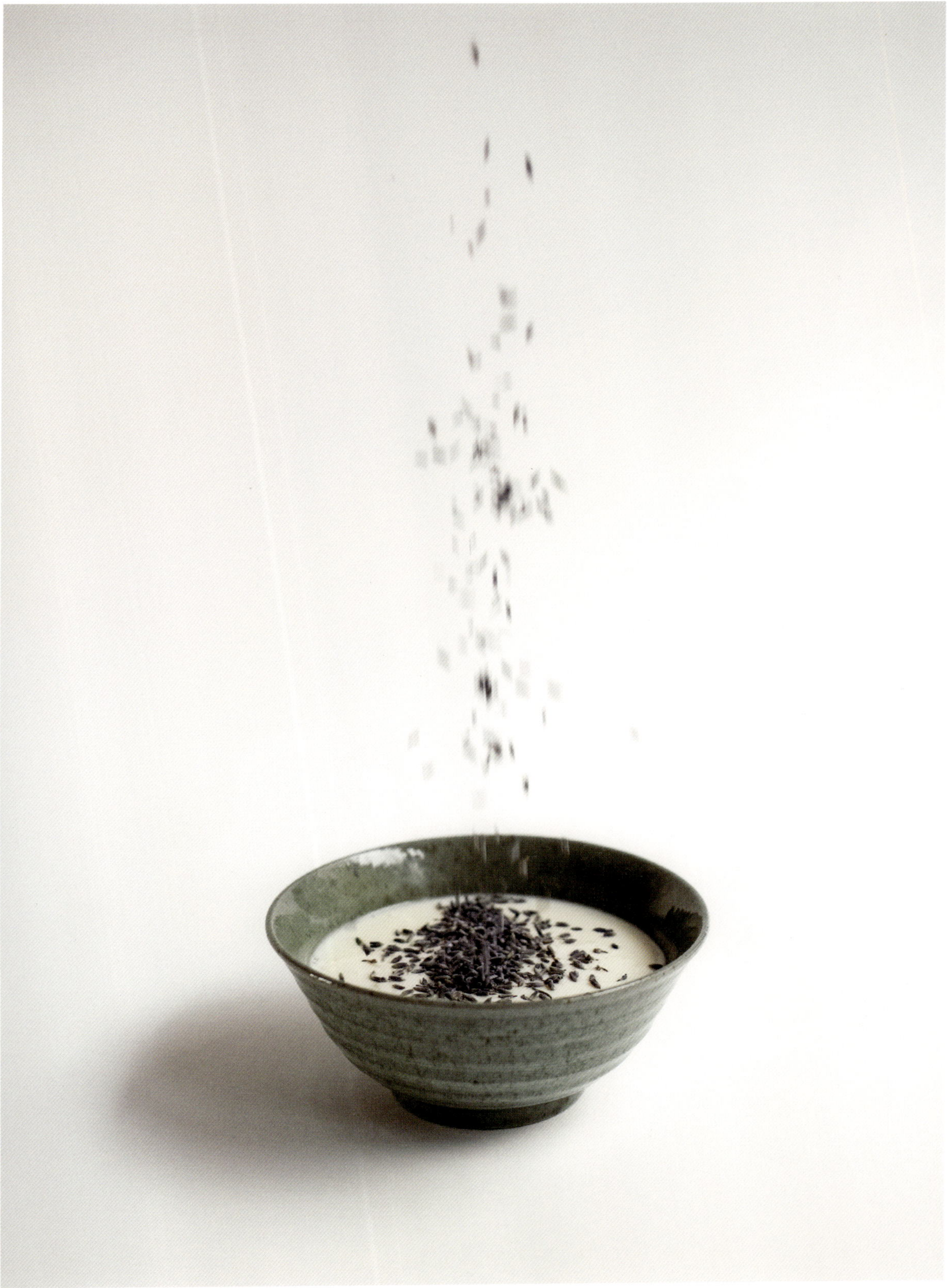

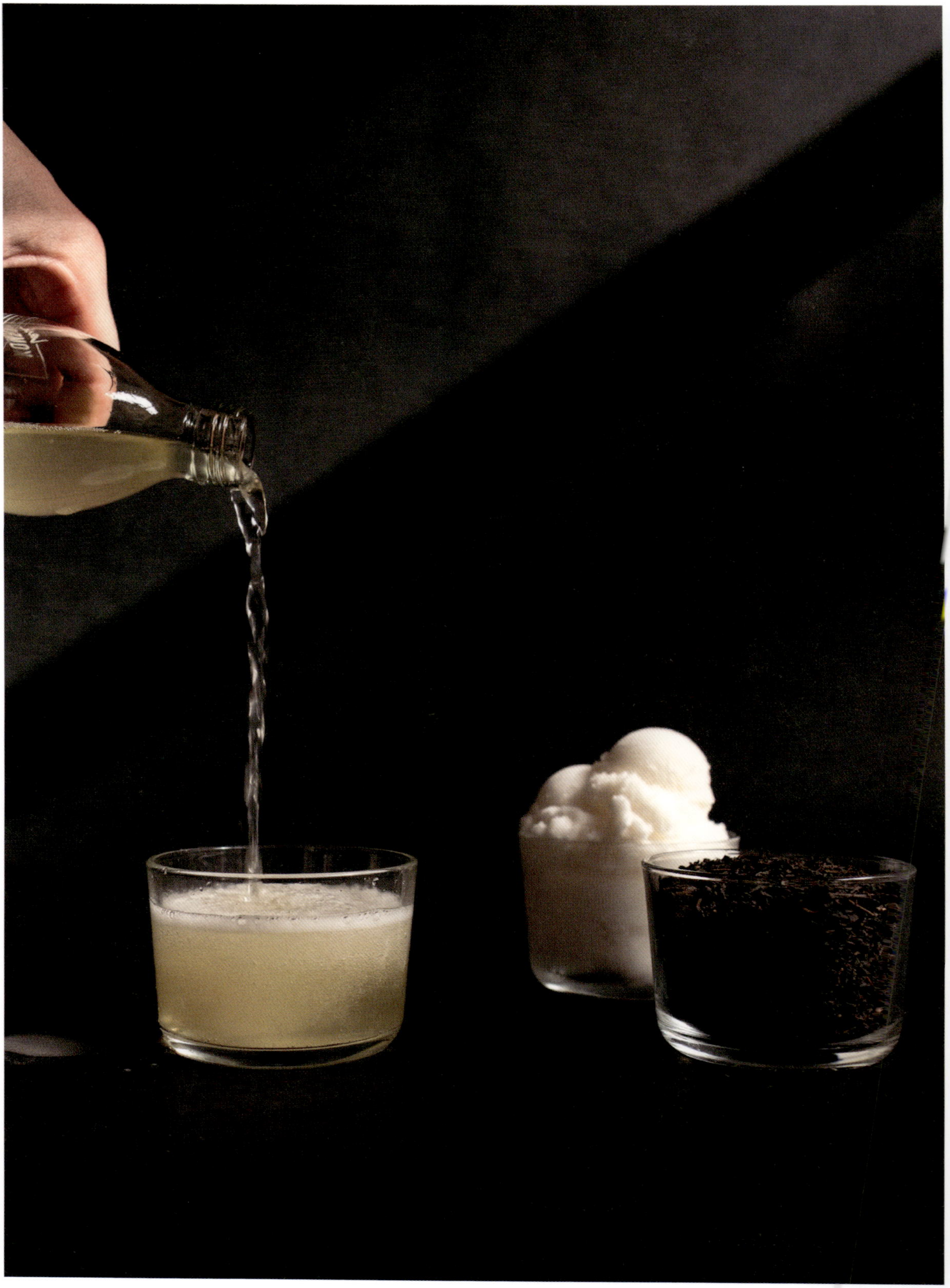

Kombucha sorbet

I am absolutely crazy about this drink. Kombucha is a fermented tea, which means that a SCOBY (symbiotic culture of bacteria and yeast) has converted most of the sugars into organic acids. The drink (when made authentically) is unpasteurised, which means the probiotic bacteria used for fermentation remain in the bottle. These probiotic bacteria and organic acids have a positive effect on your gut microbiota by introducing and encouraging the growth of beneficial bacteria.

500 g	syrup 2 *(note: only add 30 g egg white to 1 kg syrup)*
500 g	kombucha

PREPARATION

Please turn to page 23 to make the adjusted syrup 2 recipe. The acidity from Kombucha requires a syrup with less egg whites.

Mix the ingredients and freeze.

Tonka bean

Two regular customers kept talking about these so called tonka beans, and insisted I got my hands on them (thank you Andreas and Marie!). Once I surrendered and made an ice cream out of them, I knew it was there to stay. It almost tastes like a fruity and spicy marzipan combined with cinnamon and vanilla notes.

1000 g	base 2
3	tonka beans

PREPARATION Grate the tonka beans finely and add the tonka beans to the base and freeze. It is beneficial to add the grated tonka beans as you are producing the base; that way you get to pasteurise the beans.

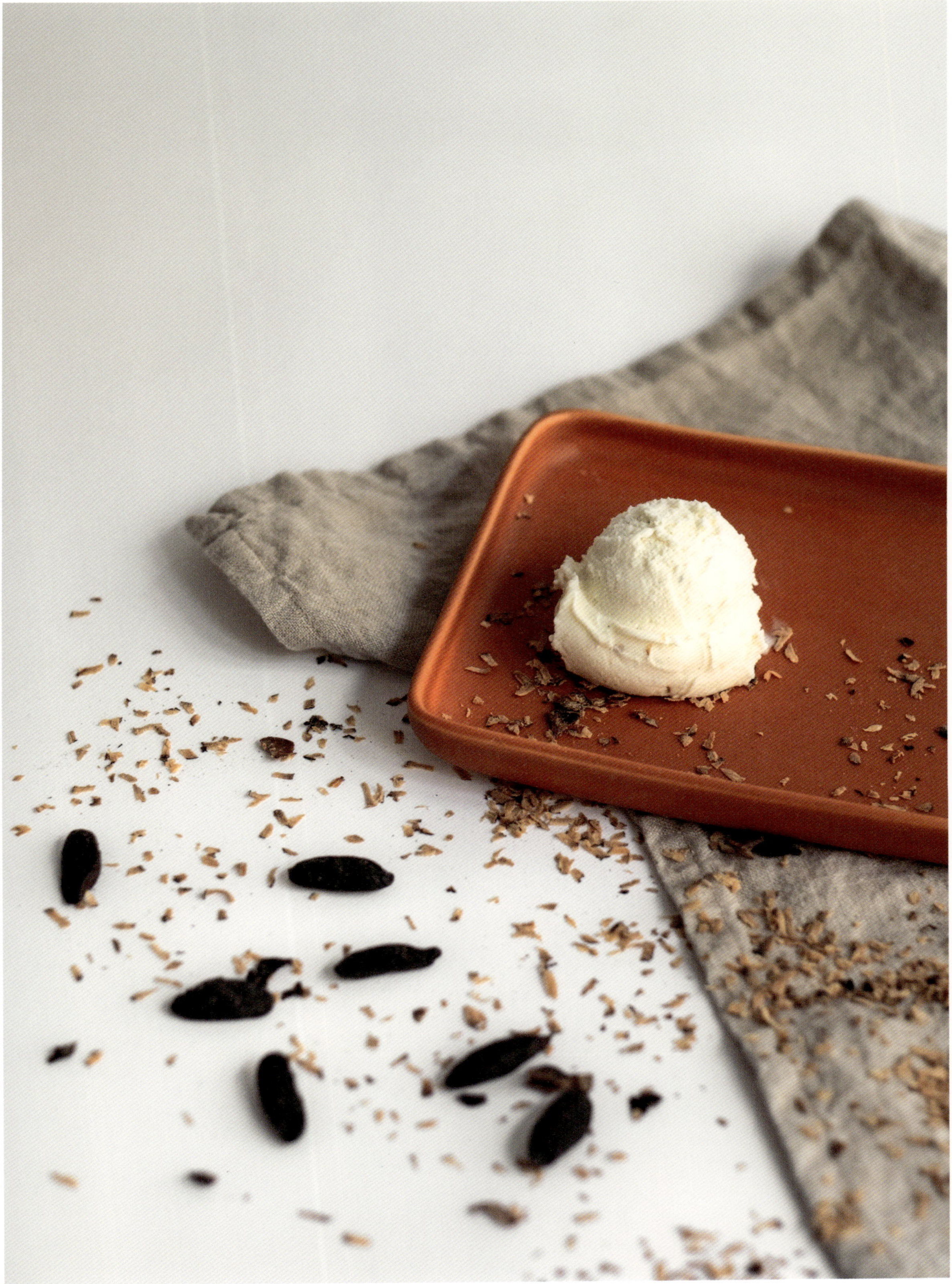

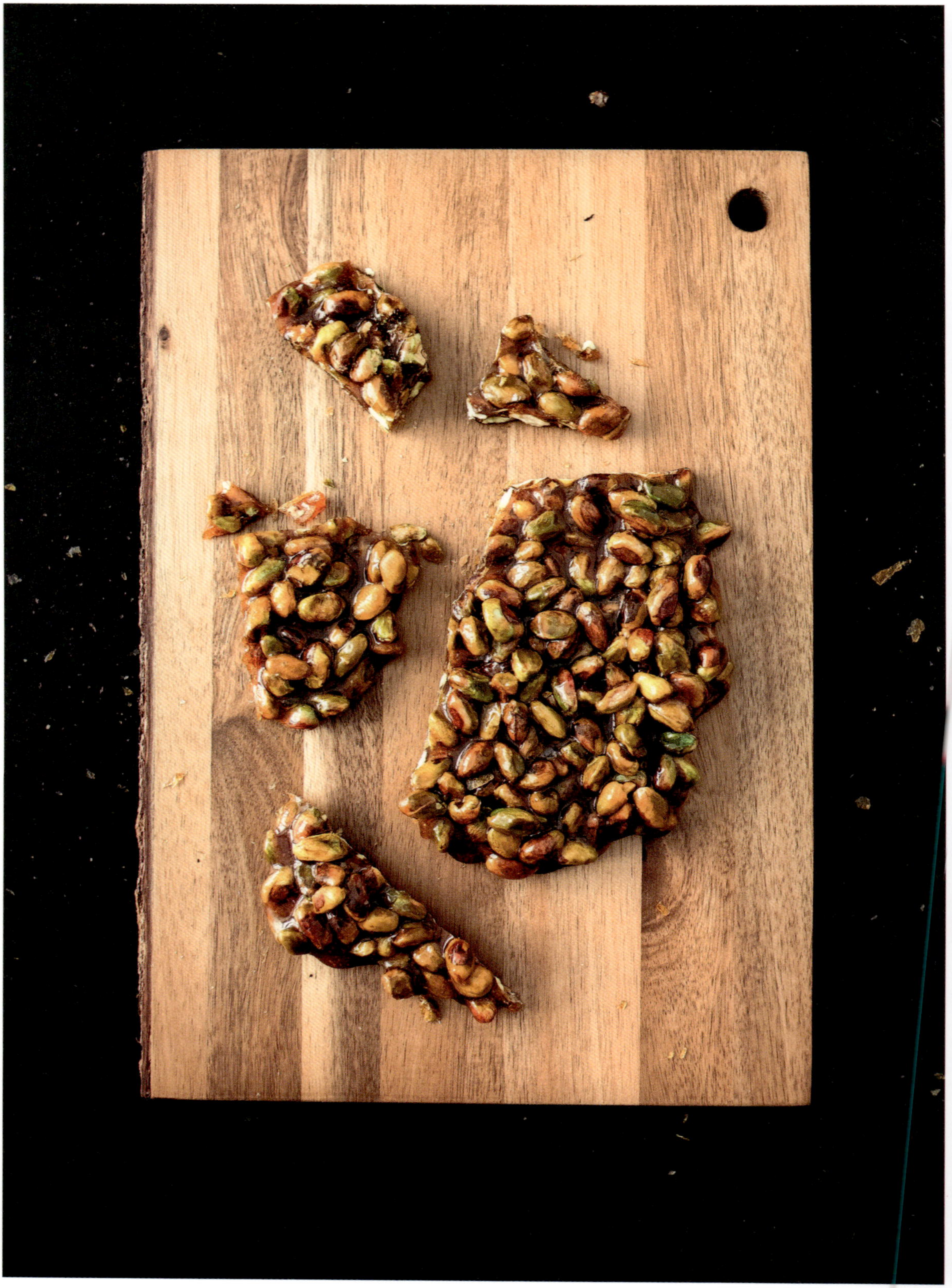

Pistachio

"Do not judge a book by its cover" (except for this one which I think looks perfect).

But please do judge a pistachio ice cream by its colour. If you see a VERY green pistachio ice cream I want your inner alarm bells to go off. Often this is the result of green colourings being added to the recipe that can consequently alter the flavour profile that follows – and this is not necessarily the best ice cream experience. Because of this, pistachio ice cream was never on my list of favourites and I never liked it at all. Until I made this recipe.

Now I cannot get enough of it. Roasting the pistachio nuts gives a completely different flavour and the colour becomes more brown in tone. When people see the brown colour, they say: that is not pistachio?! When I let them taste it, they are convinced, and I explain that the nuts are roasted and that there has been no green colouring added to the ice cream. So next time you see a pistachio ice cream, please think about this.

900 g   base 3, variety A
100 g   pistachio paste *(see recipe page 104)*

PREPARATION   Blend the base and the pistachio paste together and freeze.

Cashew nut

This recipe was developed in Vietnam. I was working on flavours, and I needed to source hazelnuts. I went to several stores and for the obvious reason that cashew nuts are grown in Vietnam, all I could find was cashew nuts. I decided to buy them with the thought that the principle was the same: the nuts would get roasted, blended and hopefully create a nice structure and flavour. I was pleasantly surprised to taste the sweet, mild cashew nuts in this ice cream. I also took the recipe to Denmark, where it became quite popular.

900 g	base 3, variety A
100 g	cashew nut paste *(see page 104 for nut pastes)*

PREPARATION Blend the ingredients together and freeze.

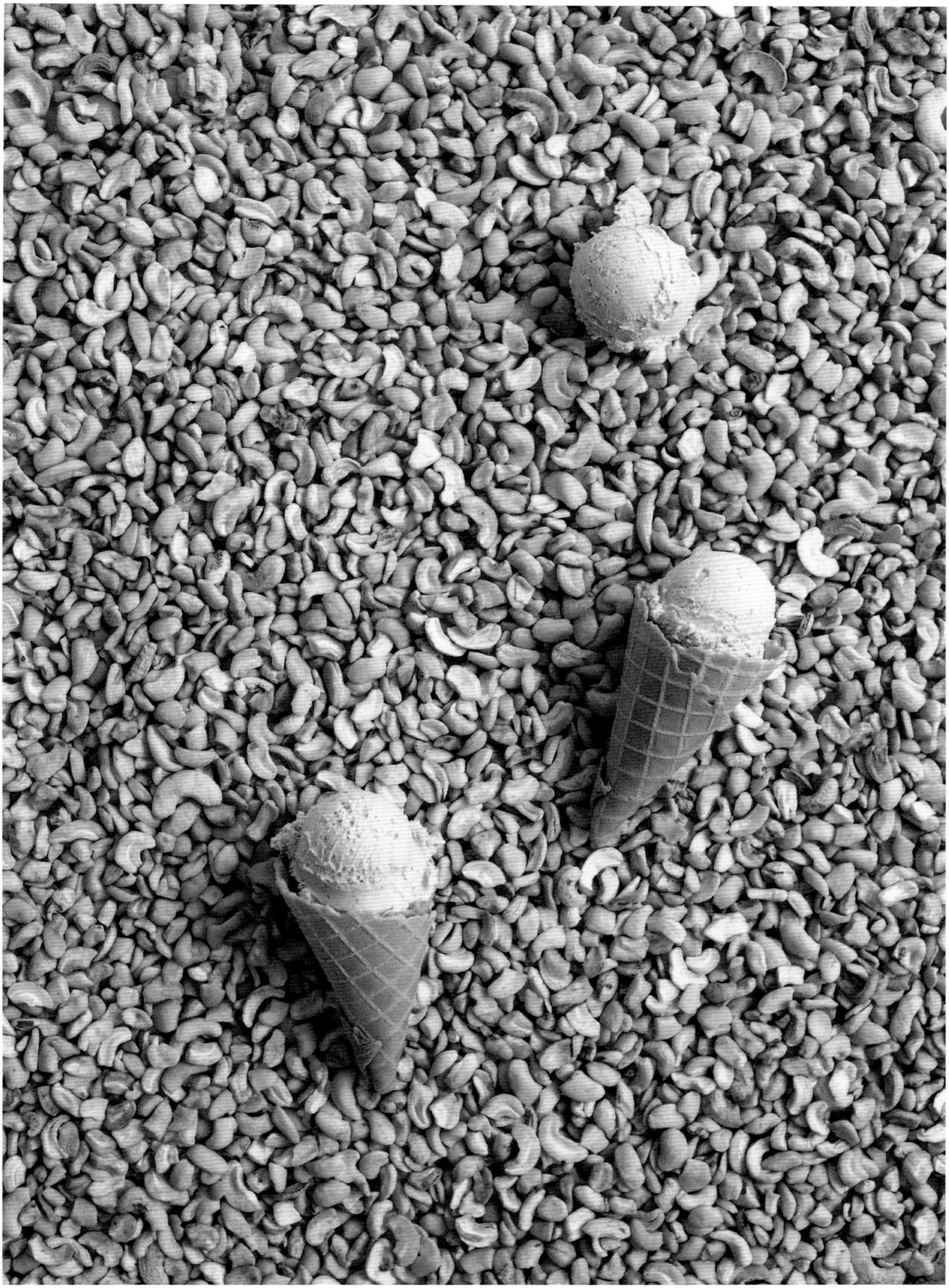

Hazelnut

Creating ice creams with nuts require a bit of work, but I really believe it is worth it. Both the hazelnut paste and the ice cream taste like something I want to consume nonstop!

900 g   base 3, variety A
100 g   hazelnut paste *(see recipe page 104)*

PREPARATION   Blend the base and the hazelnut paste together and freeze.

unroasted hazelnuts

roasted hazelnuts

hazelnut nougat

hazelnut
paste

hazelnut
ice cream

Maple & walnut

Since studying ice cream science in the Canadian town of Guelph, Canada has a big place in my heart. Furthermore, having had a colleague, Emily, from Canada resulted in the development of an ice cream almost like this. Maple syrup is mandatory in a Canadian inspired flavour together with some caramelised pecan nuts. I just decided to use walnuts instead.

950 g	base 3, variety A *(replace all the sucrose with maple syrup)*
50 g	walnut paste *(see page 104 for recipe)*
100 g	walnut nougat *(see page 97 for recipe)*

PREPARATION Prepare the paste and the nougat. Blend the walnut paste with the base and freeze in the ice cream machine. Fold in the walnut nougat when the ice cream is scoopable.

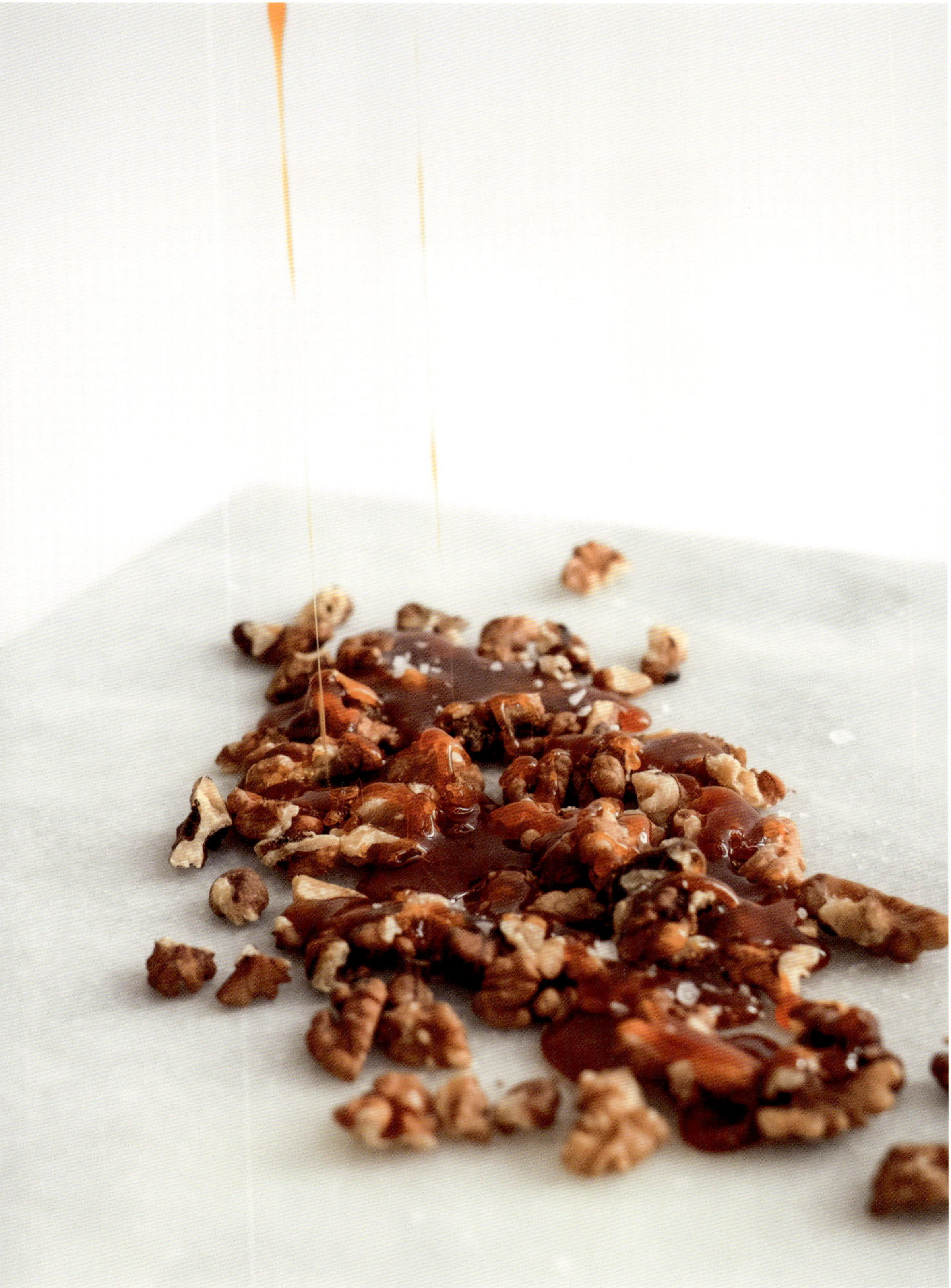

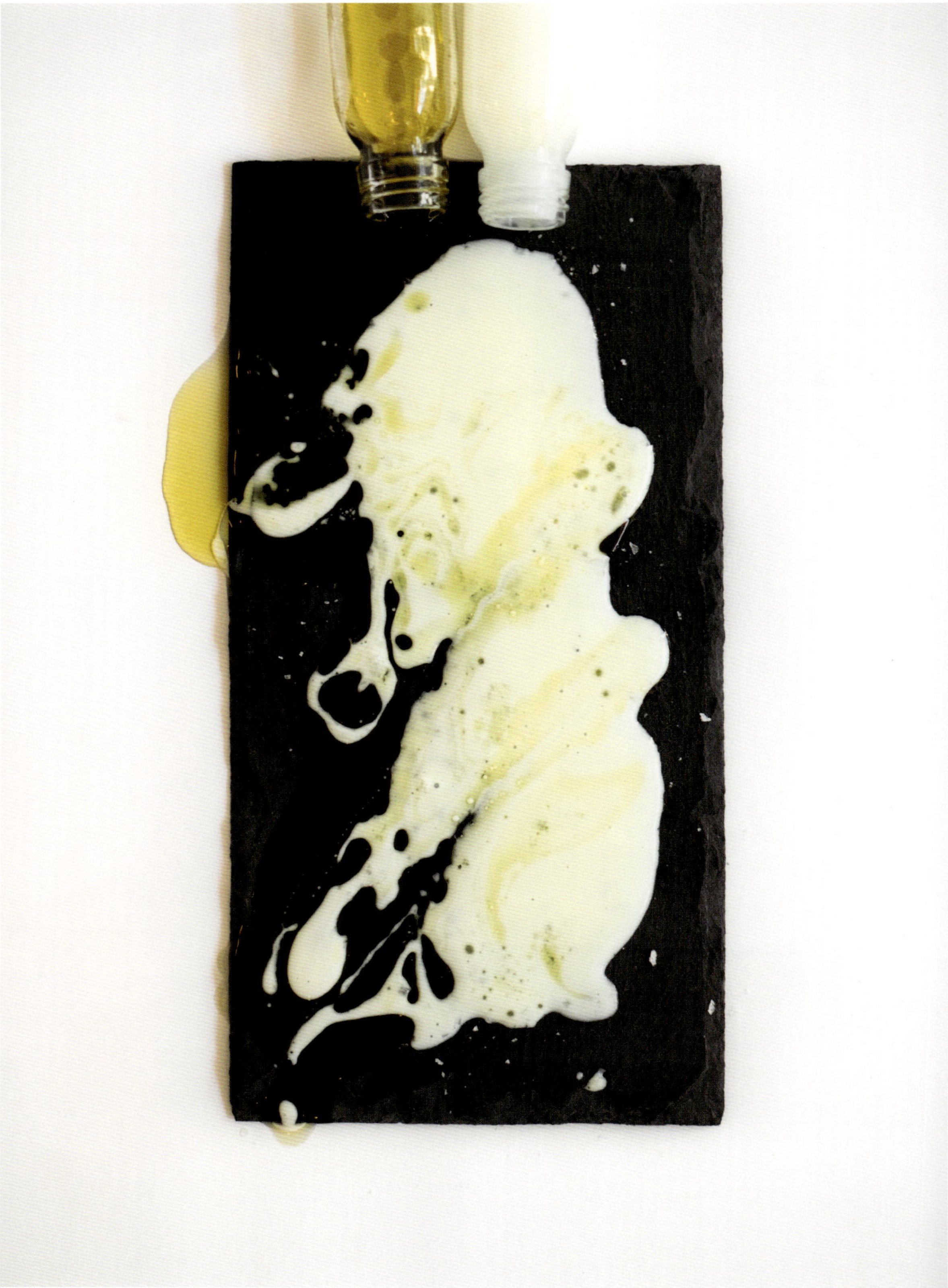

Olive oil

Olive oil of high quality has a spicy and aromatic flavour, which goes really well in an ice cream. I recommend using a base with a relatively low-fat content because there is quite a lot of fat added from the olive oil. If you are adventurous, you could make some small ryebread croutons and serve them on the side so you can dip the crispy bread in the ice cream.

900 g	base 2
50–100 g	olive oil
1 pinch	sea salt

PREPARATION Combine all the ingredients, starting with 50 g of olive oil. Keep adding enough olive oil until you think the flavour is strong enough. The amount of olive oil depends on your choice of oil and how strong a flavour you want. When you are happy with the flavour, freeze it.

Ginger & chili

I have always liked this combination because of the contrasts: spicy and sweet, hot and cold, intense and mild, pungent and soothing. Another interesting aspect is also how the ginger flavour comes out first, and once the milk and cream is completely out of the mouth, you start feeling the capsaicin pungency on your tongue from the chili. A complex ice cream you could call it.

1000 g	base 3, variety C
40 g	red chili
60 g	ginger

PREPARATION Remove most of the seeds from the chili and peel the ginger.

Blend the chili and ginger in a small food processor until it is a homogenous paste. Mix it with the base and freeze.

If you do not like the bits and pieces from the chili and ginger, you can strain it, but I find that it loses some of its pungency and character by straining it.

Pumpkin spice

Inspired from Northern America, this recipe requires a lot of tasting of the mix to get the right balance between pumpkin and spices.

900 g	base 3, variety A
150 g	hokkaido pumpkin
10 g	butter
3 tsp	ground cinnamon
¼ tsp	ground cloves
¼ tsp	ground nutmeg
½ tsp	ground ginger
1 pinch	chili powder
1 pinch	sea salt

PREPARATION Cut the pumpkin into smaller pieces (2–3 cm), put them on a baking tray and rub them in the butter and 1 tsp. cinnamon. Bake the pumpkin for 45 minutes at 175°C or until soft. Let the pumpkin cool down and blend it together with the base and the spices. Taste it as you go, and add more of whatever spice you wish until you think it has a good balanced flavour. Freeze it.

Pumpkin contains a good amount of water and fibres, so I recommend you to use the base containing dextrose to make it softer. Alternatively, use any of the other bases and add 50 g dextrose.

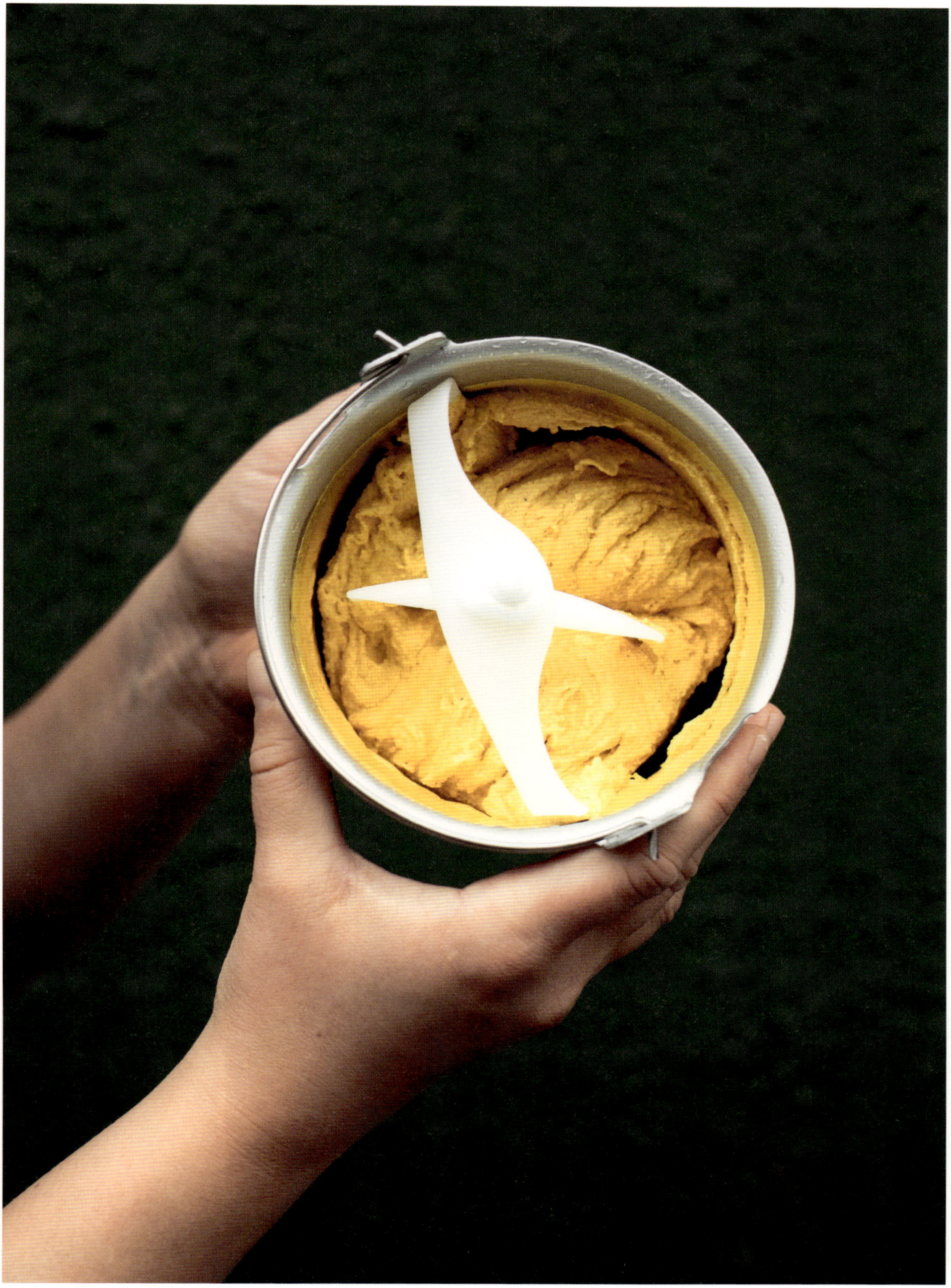

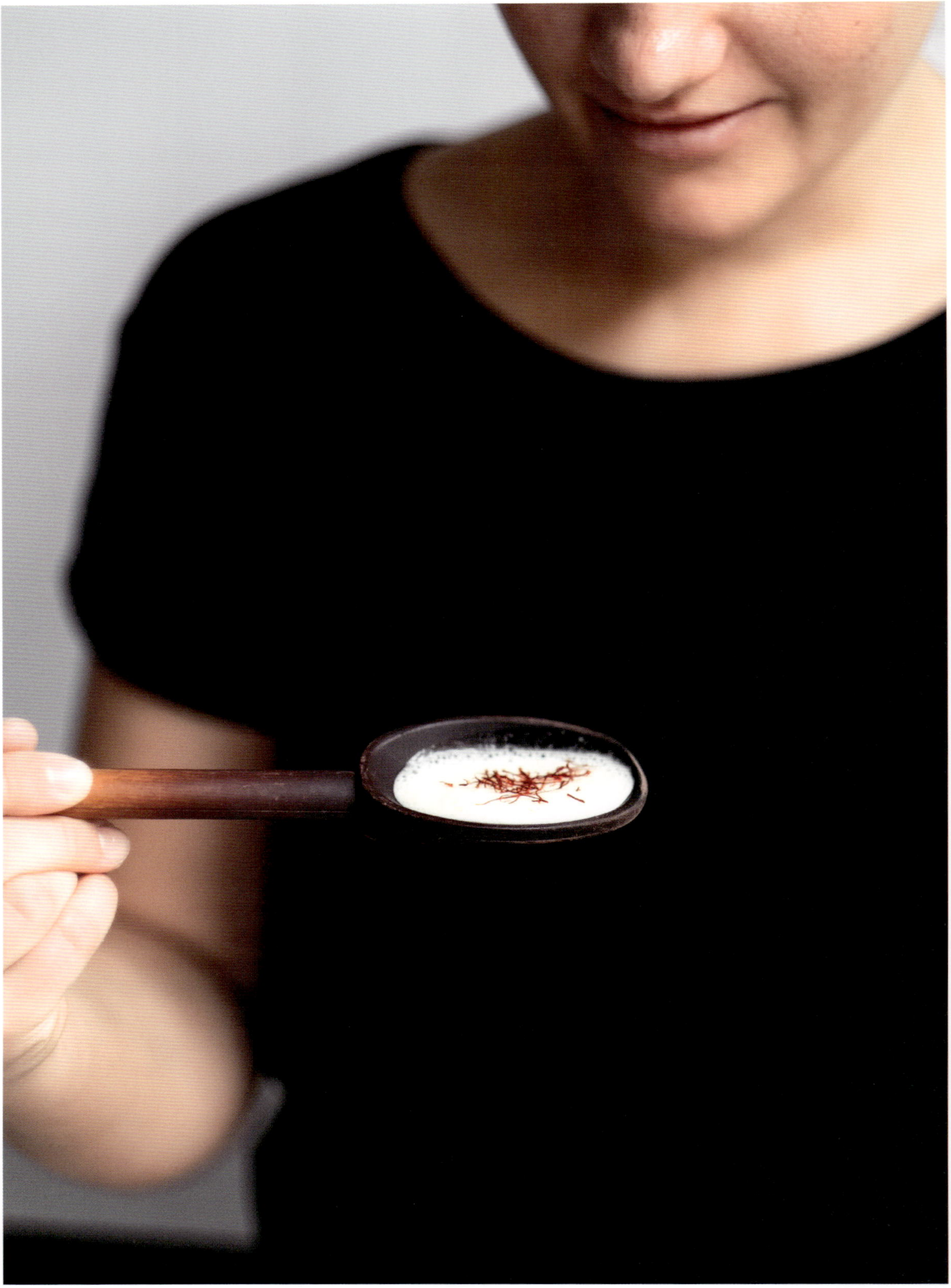

Saffron & honey

My colleague Matilde came up with the idea to this recipe and created it. The ice cream sold out fast and got a lot of great feedback, so hopefully you will like it too. The sweet, flowery notes from the honey combined with the delicate aromas of saffron is amazing!

1000 g	base, variety B *(add 80 g honey instead of glucose in the base recipe)*
1 tsp	saffron
1 pinch	salt

PREPARATION Blend everything together, leave for 30 minutes to let the saffron flavours develop, and freeze. Like with many other things, the higher the quality (of saffron) you use, the better the flavour.

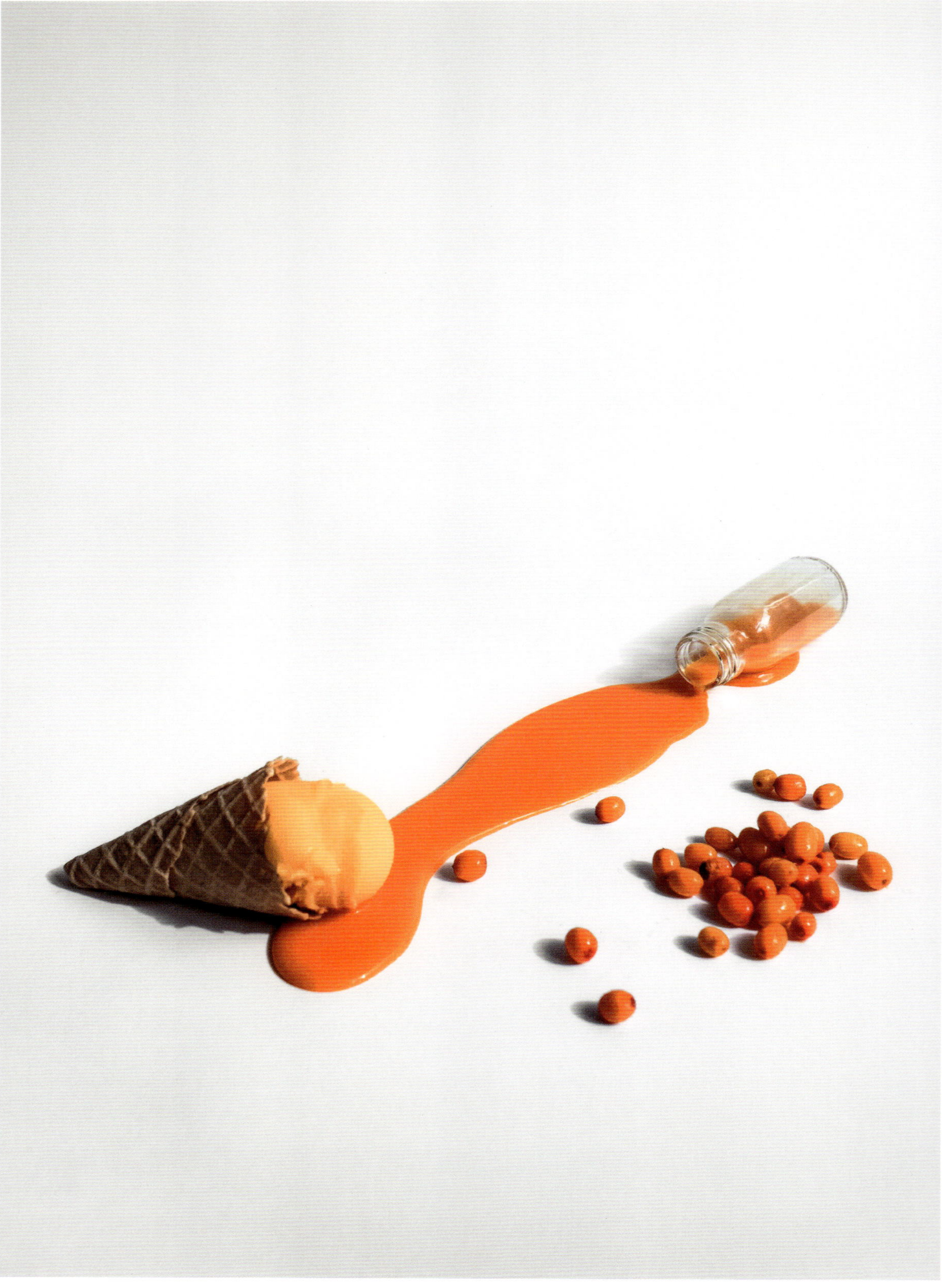

Sea buckthorn sorbet

There is so much good to say about sea buckthorn. I wrote my bachelor thesis on the fatty acids in sea buckthorn, so when someone asks me what it is, I reply back: how much time do you have? The health benefits of sea buckthorn is a field worth studying because of its high amount of antioxidants and content of omega 3, 6, 7 and 9 fatty acids (this is very untraditional for a berry).

But none of that matters here, because the fantastic flavour of sea buckthorn is enough. The fresh and sharp flavour profile is excellent when it is combined with a sweet sorbet syrup. The type of sea buckthorn you choose will influence if it gets bitter or tart, so you might have to try various types if you can. Alternatively, try to source a good sea buckthorn juice and use that.

500 g	sorbet syrup 3, variety C
250 g	sea buckthorn or juice
250 g	water

PREPARATION Blend everything together and strain away the seeds/skin. Freeze.

Caramelised grapefruit sorbet

This recipe is the work of one of my first regular customers, who later became an ice cream girl in the shops and now she is my good friend. Marie has always had an abundance of ideas for ice creams and desserts, which was how we first bonded.

500 g	syrup 2 *(note: only add 20 g egg whites/kg)*
500 g	juice from grapefruits *(~5–6 grapefruits)*
10 g	sucrose
1 tsp	cinnamon
1 pinch	salt

PREPARATION Cut the grapefruit in halves and place on a baking sheet.

Preheat the oven for broil. Meanwhile mix sucrose, cinnamon and salt and sprinkle it onto the grapefruits (not on the skin – onto the juicy part). Broil the grapefruits for 5 minutes until the sucrose-mix is golden brown and caramelised. Let the grapefruits cool down and then squeeze the juice out. Weigh off 500 g and blend with the syrup. Feel free to add either salt or a bit of lemon to get the perfect balance. Freeze.

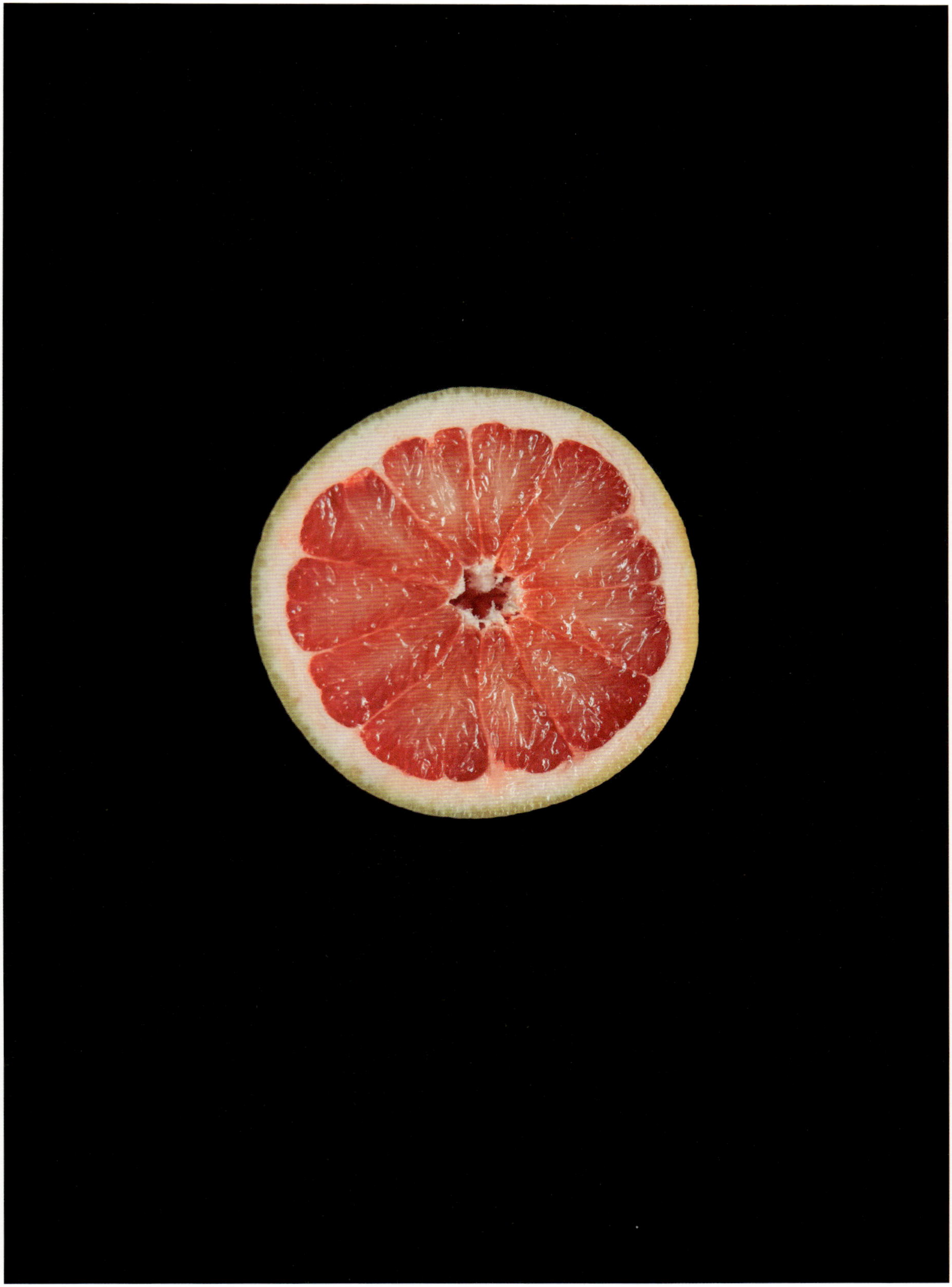

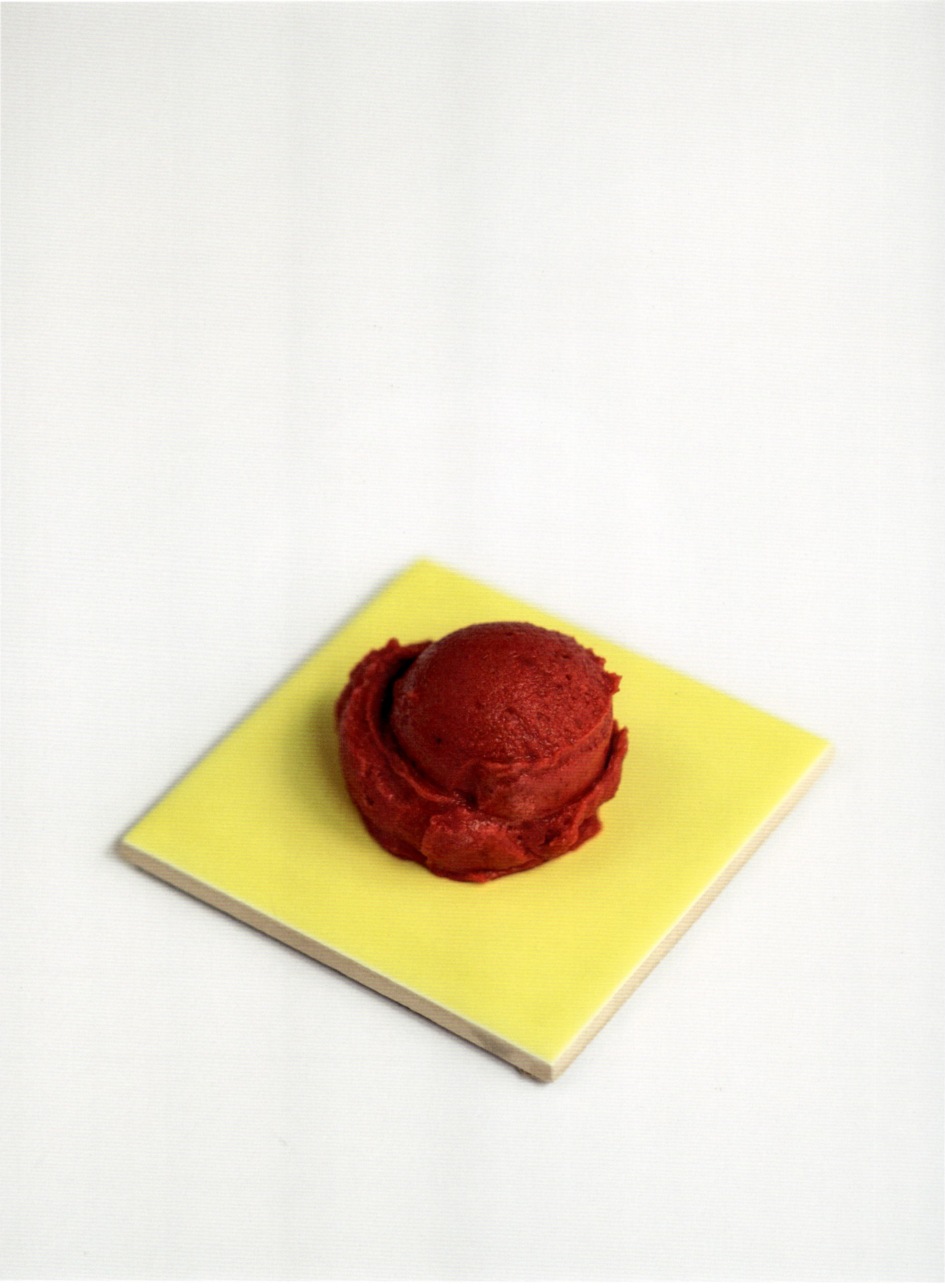

Cherry sorbet

I like to use either black or sour cherries for this recipe to get a very fresh sorbet. This recipe is a very basic sorbet recipe, because you can replace the cherries with more or less any kind of berries: blueberries, raspberries, gooseberries, blackberries, strawberries and so on. They all get a very intense flavour because 50% fruit is added.

500 g	sorbet syrup 2
500 g	cherries

PREPARATION Depit the cherries and boil them in a pot until they are soft and like a compote. Cool them down and blend together with the syrup. You can now choose to strain the mix or keep the pieces of skin in the mix. It depends on whether you like some pieces or not. Freeze.

Banana sorbet

For the past couple of years, I have heard so much about bananas you do not believe it. The reason for this is that my father is involved in starting an organic banana farm from scratch in Kenya. His passion for this is out of this world. I have learned a lot about bananas and the many challenges involved, how this can generate a great living for the farmers and much more. I am totally backing up this project by suggesting you make a banana sorbet.

500 g	sorbet syrup 2
500 g	banana pulp
10 g	lemon juice

PREPARATION Select the bananas when they are perfectly ripe. Trial and error...

Blend the three ingredients together and taste the mix. If it needs more lemon, now is the time to add this. The level of lemon depends on the ripeness of the bananas. Freeze.

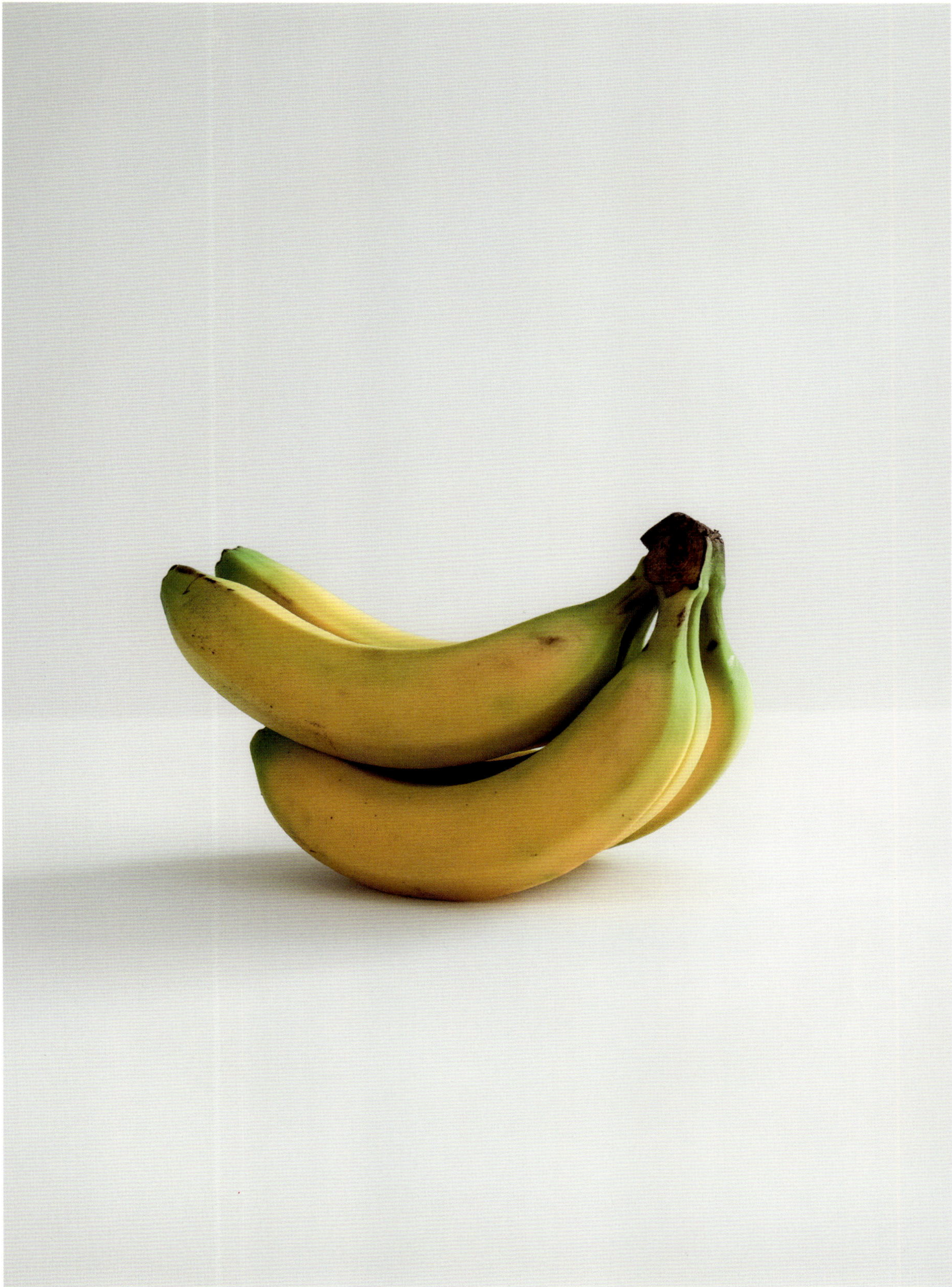

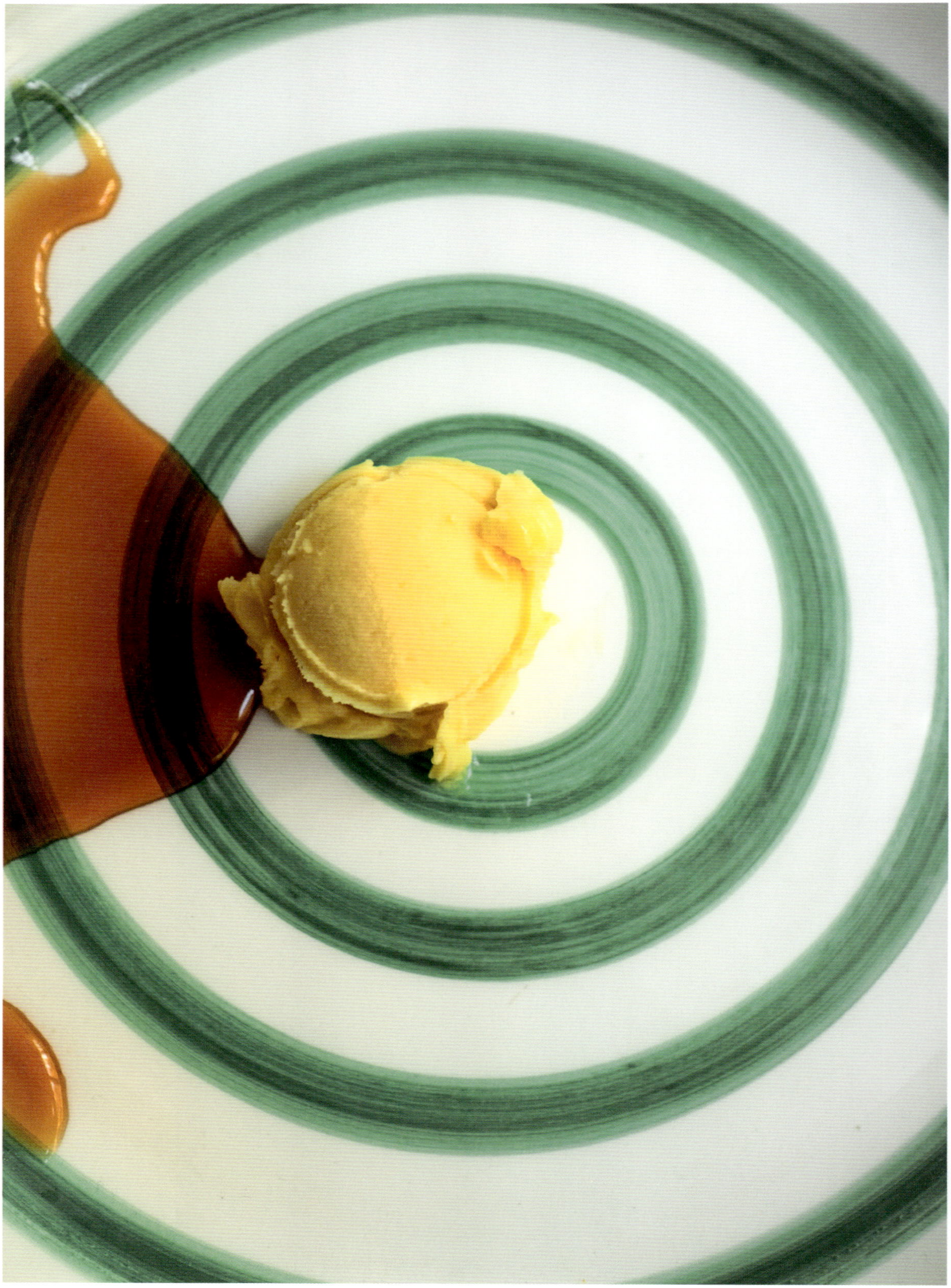

Mango & coconut palm syrup

The caramel notes from using coconut palm syrup as the only source of sugar to this recipe add some nice flavour pairings to the mango. You can either use it as the liquid syrup or as dry coconut sugar. Regardless it will taste like being in the Asian part of the world enjoying a scoop of mango sorbet.

I called my father if he had any suggestion for the variety of mangoes. The answer was: Apple Mango from Kenya (it could sound like he is about to start a mango farm in Kenya, too…). Or Alphonso would be acceptable too. There are more than 1000 varieties of mango, and it can be hard to choose.

500 g	sorbet syrup 3, variety A *(add the palm syrup as the only sugar source)*
500 g	mango pulp

PREPARATION Blend the two ingredients together (add a hint of lemon if you find it too sweet) and freeze.

Liquorice

We Danes love our liquorice. As candy, as a syrup or powder to sprinkle on our cakes, and of course in ice cream. I prefer the liquorice to be milder and sweeter like the actual liquorice roots. And quite a lot of visitors from outside of Denmark have not been completely disgusted by this recipe. But in Vietnam the locals do think this is a bit of a weird flavour. Just like we Danes think durian is odd. It just underlines the fact that taste preferences are also based on culture and exposure.

1000 g	base 2
10 g	liquorice powder

PREPARATION Blend the two ingredients and freeze.

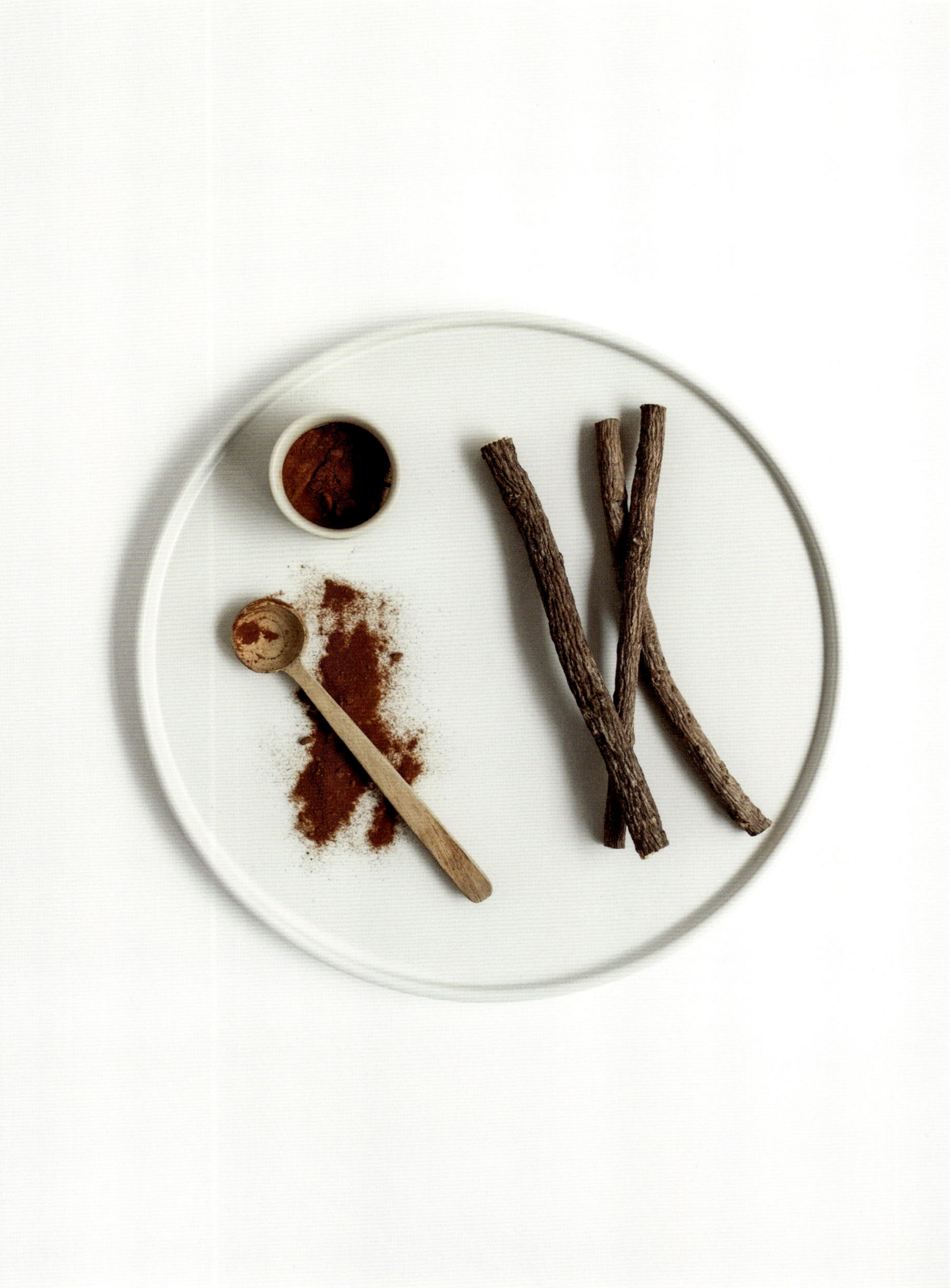

Strawberry

This is the taste of a Danish summer to me. Go into the fields, pick your own strawberries and make this ice cream. It does not get much better than that! I recommend using the strawberry variety called corona. It gives a very fruity, round and aromatic flavour. If you trust your strawberry supplier, I recommend using the berries fresh. If you go for frozen strawberries it is always a good idea to boil them. The flavour profile of boiled berries is just a little bit different and more towards the cooked notes – so I recommend you use them fresh if you feel comfortable with that. On a professional scale I would never take that chance. Safety first.

265 g	cream
185 g	skimmed milk
100 g	sucrose
70 g	skimmed milk powder
40 g	glucose syrup
40 g	egg yolks
2 g	locust bean gum
300 g	strawberries

PREPARATION

Heat up cream, skimmed milk, sucrose, skimmed milk powder, glucose syrup, egg yolks and locust bean gum in a heavy-bottomed pot under constant stirring until it reaches 85°C. Blend it really well, cool down to 5°C in an ice bath and leave to age in the fridge.

Blend the base together with the rinsed or boiled strawberries. If you want a more acidic ice cream, add a squeeze of lemon juice. Freeze.

SCIENCE NOTES

The composition for this recipe is:

30% strawberries, 16% total sugars ,10% dairy fat, 10% MSNF, 4% egg yolks

I have considered the amount of sugars coming from strawberries. So, in this case, the amount of added sugars is 14%. Strawberries usually contain 8–10% sugars, so we have added around 2% sugar coming from the berries.

Most other fruits can be used in this recipe instead of strawberries. The concept is similar to the espresso/beer/Irish cream recipe. In this one you can just add up to 30% fruit/ingredient.

Strawberry sorbet

Just like for the ice cream, I recommend using the corona sort for this sorbet. The advantage of making strawberry sorbet is that it gets a much more intense strawberry flavour due to the high amount of strawberries used. Strawberries contain fibres, which is also the reason it becomes very creamy. So, when you think about it, this is actually a good way to get some healthy fruit into your diet...

500 g	sorbet syrup 2
500 g	strawberries
5 g	lemon juice

PREPARATION Either just rinse the strawberries and blend them with the syrup and the lemon juice or give them a quick boil. If you are using frozen strawberries, I recommend you give them a quick boil. Freeze.

This recipe is valid for most other berries (but you do not have to add the lemon juice): raspberries, blueberries, blackberries, gooseberries and so on.

Rhubarb sorbet

This sorbet is very fresh due to the high acidity from rhubarbs and rich in structure due to the fact that rhubarb contains dietary fibres. It is important to boil the rhubarbs really well to break down the structure so there are not too many threads left in the sorbet. Alternatively, you can strain it before freezing.

500 g	sorbet syrup 2
500 g	rhubarb

PREPARATION Boil the rhubarb really well until it is like a purée (this might take an hour with constant stirring). Blend together with the syrup until smooth and freeze.

The egg white content is not adjusted despite the high acidity in rhubarbs. This is because the rhubarb sorbet is quite "heavy" in structure, so it needs a high air incorporation.

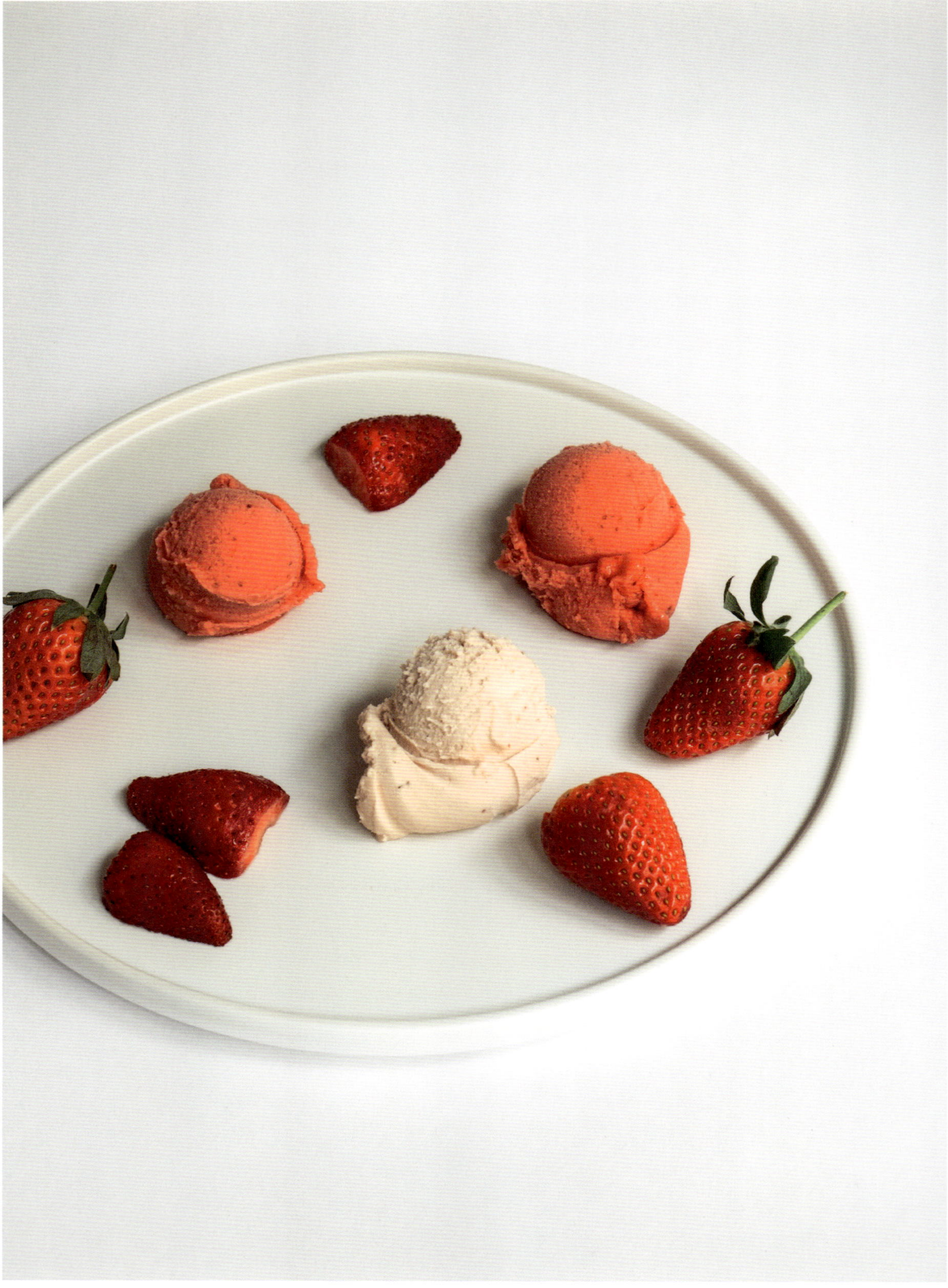

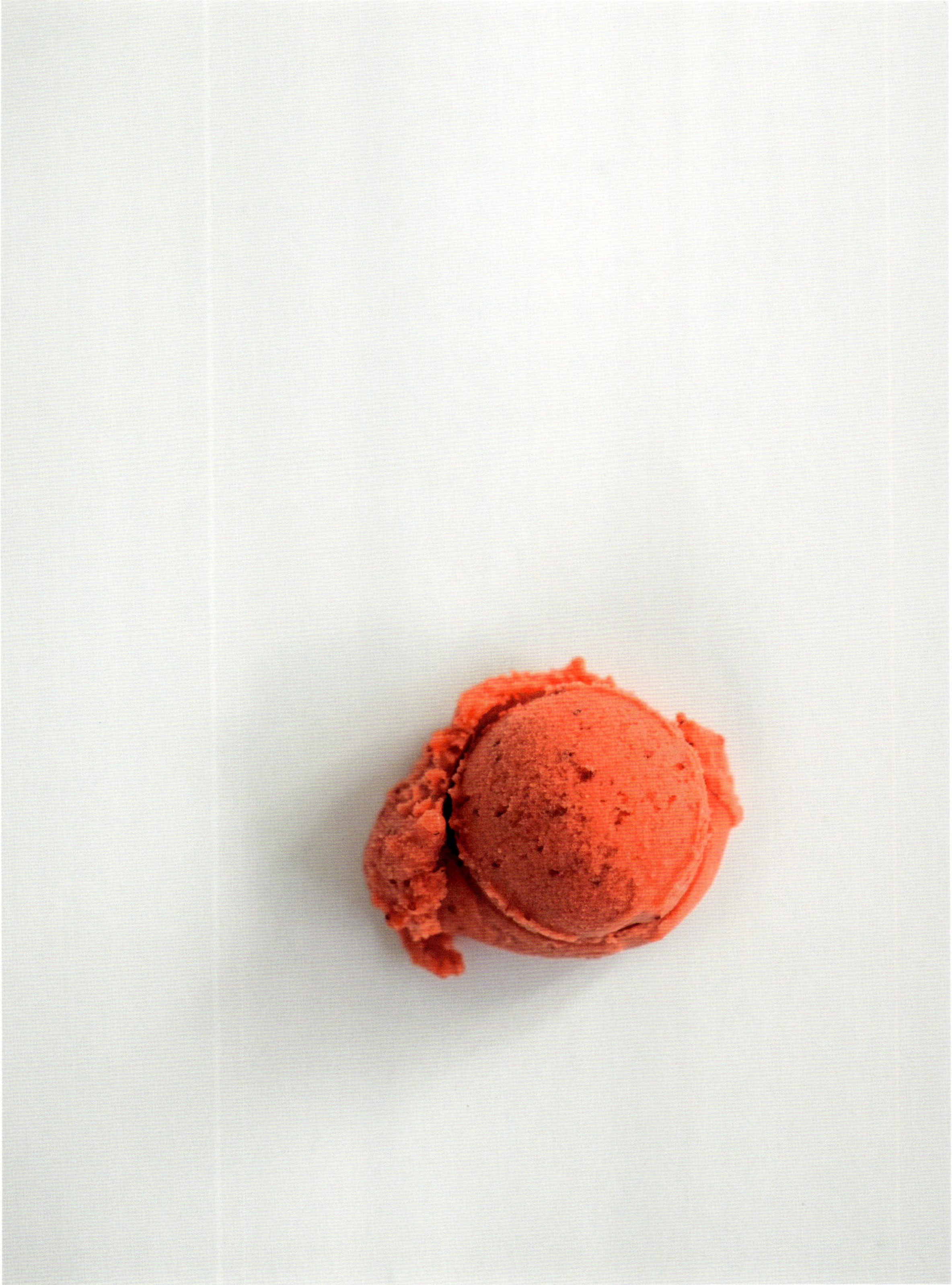

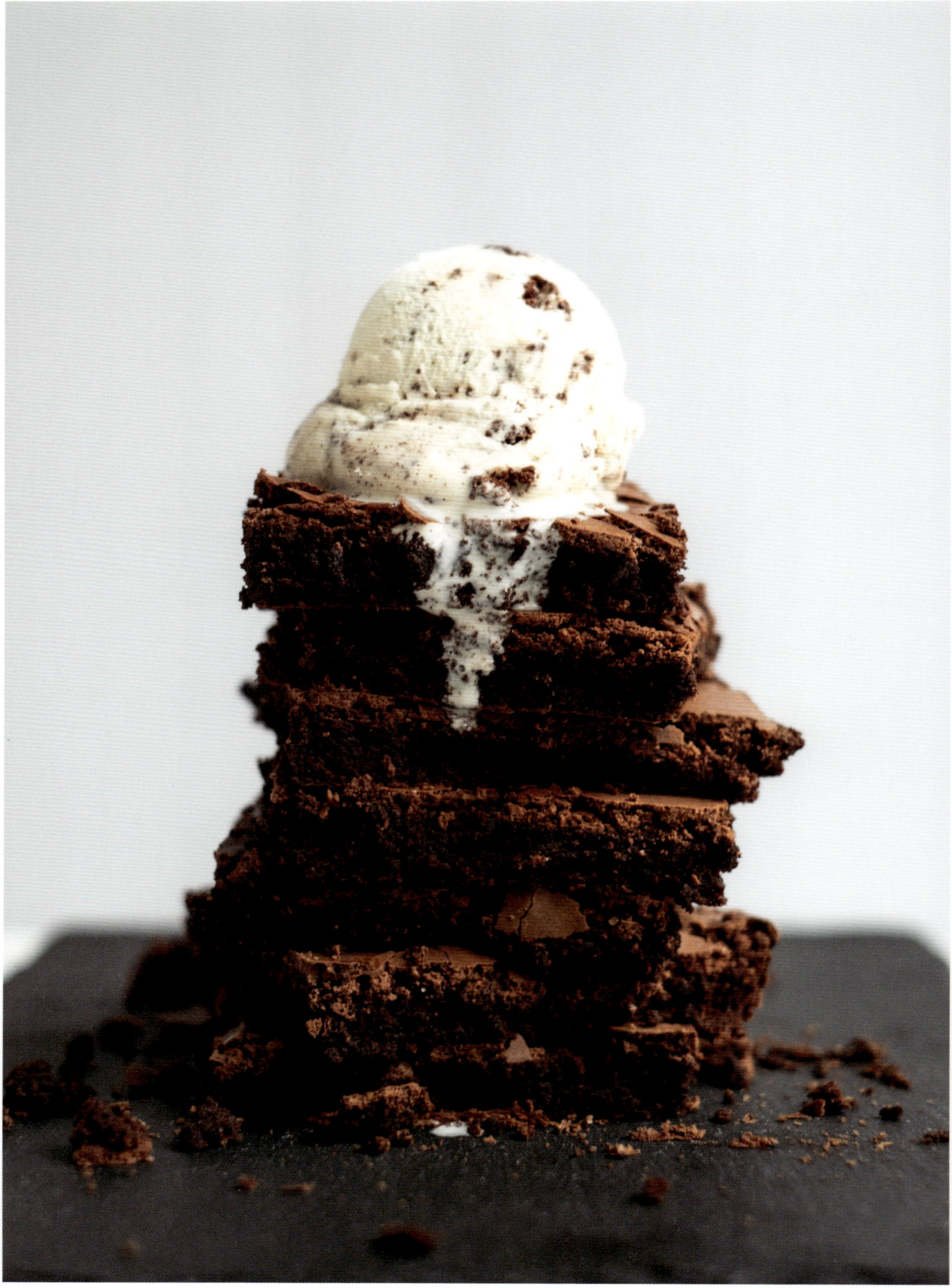

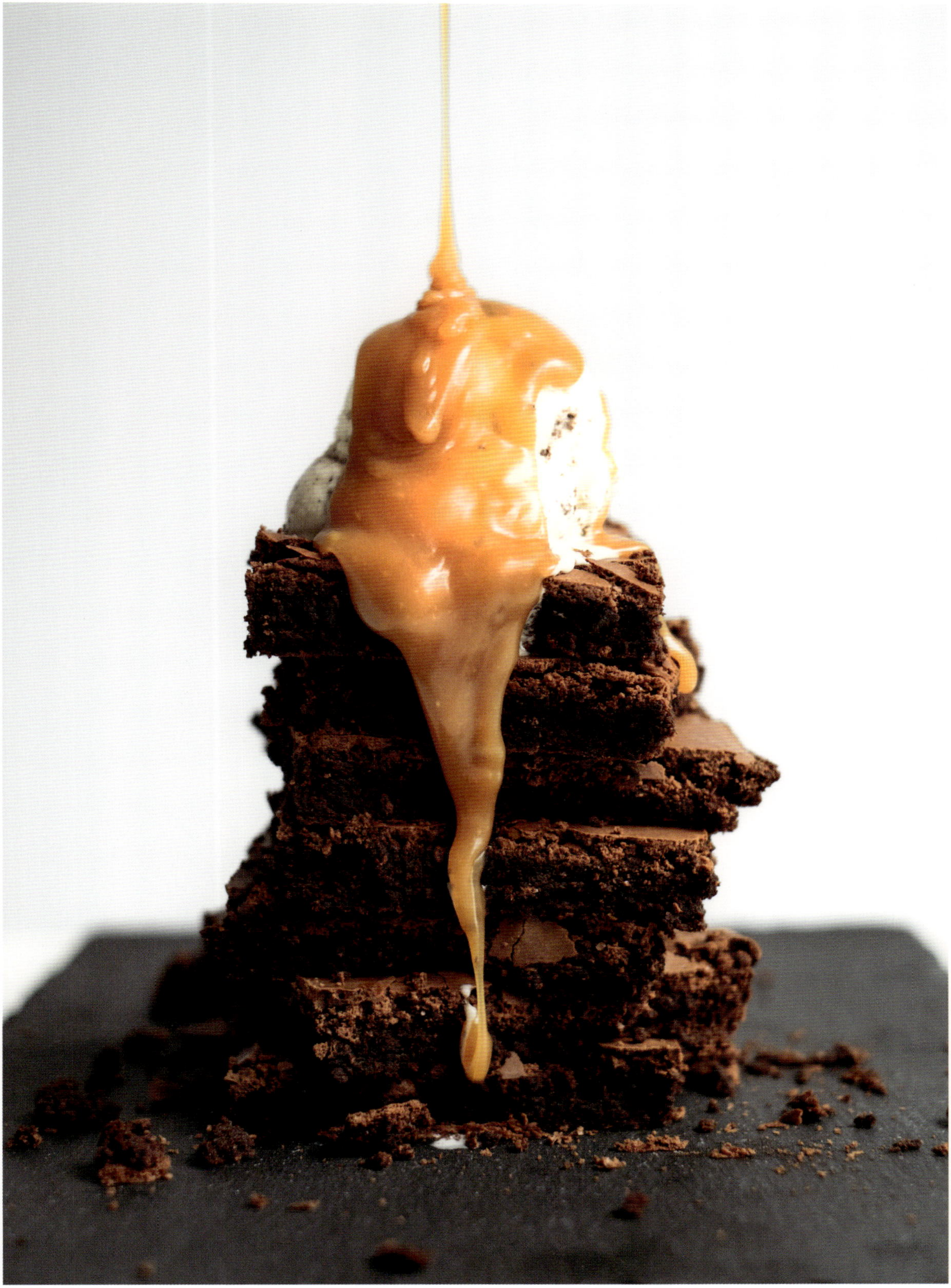

Brownie

This brownie is perfect if you want to add it as pieces to ice cream, but even just baking it to serve a piece on the side of some ice cream or sorbet is an excellent idea (if I should say so myself).

100 g	butter
200 g	dark chocolate
285 g	sucrose
4	eggs
50 g	wheat flour
15 g	cocoa powder
1 tsp	baking powder
1 pinch	salt

PREPARATION Melt the butter and the chocolate in a pot until it is homogenous. Let it cool down to room temperature. Preheat the oven to 170°C convection. Whip the eggs and the sucrose until the volume is more or less doubled.

Gradually add the butter/chocolate mix to the egg/sucrose mix.
In another bowl combine flour, cocoa powder, baking powder and salt.
Sift it into the chocolate mix and gently fold together.

Line a baking tray with baking paper and pour in the brownie batter. Bake the brownie for approximately 30 minutes. I prefer it when the brownie is really sticky in the middle, but if you want it more baked, you need to keep it in the oven for another 5–10 minutes.

Let the brownie cool down, and then crumble into small pieces ready to go into the ice cream or cut it into squares for the dessert plate.

Take 1 kg of any base, add some vanilla, freeze and add the brownie pieces when the ice cream is scoopable.

Salty caramel

No words are needed to introduce this flavour. I can only strongly recommend you make the caramel sauce from scratch.

925 g	base 3, variety C
150 g	salty caramel sauce *(see below)*

PREPARATION   Make the caramel sauce well ahead of time so it is not warm when working with it.

Blend together the base and 75 g salty caramel sauce. Freeze and add the remaining 75 g salty caramel as a swirl when the ice cream is scoopable.

Salty caramel sauce

It is so good I could eat it with a spoon straight from the pot.

100 g	sucrose
20 g	butter
100 g	cream
1 tsp	sea salt

PREPARATION   Heat the sucrose and butter together in a pot, stirring it until the sucrose is completely dissolved and the mixture has turned to a caramel brown colour (approximately 10 minutes at medium heat). Stir in the cream and salt and take it off the heat.

If you need to, you can blend it and cool down in the fridge.

If you do not want a salty caramel sauce, just add a pinch of salt to the above recipe instead of the 1 tsp.

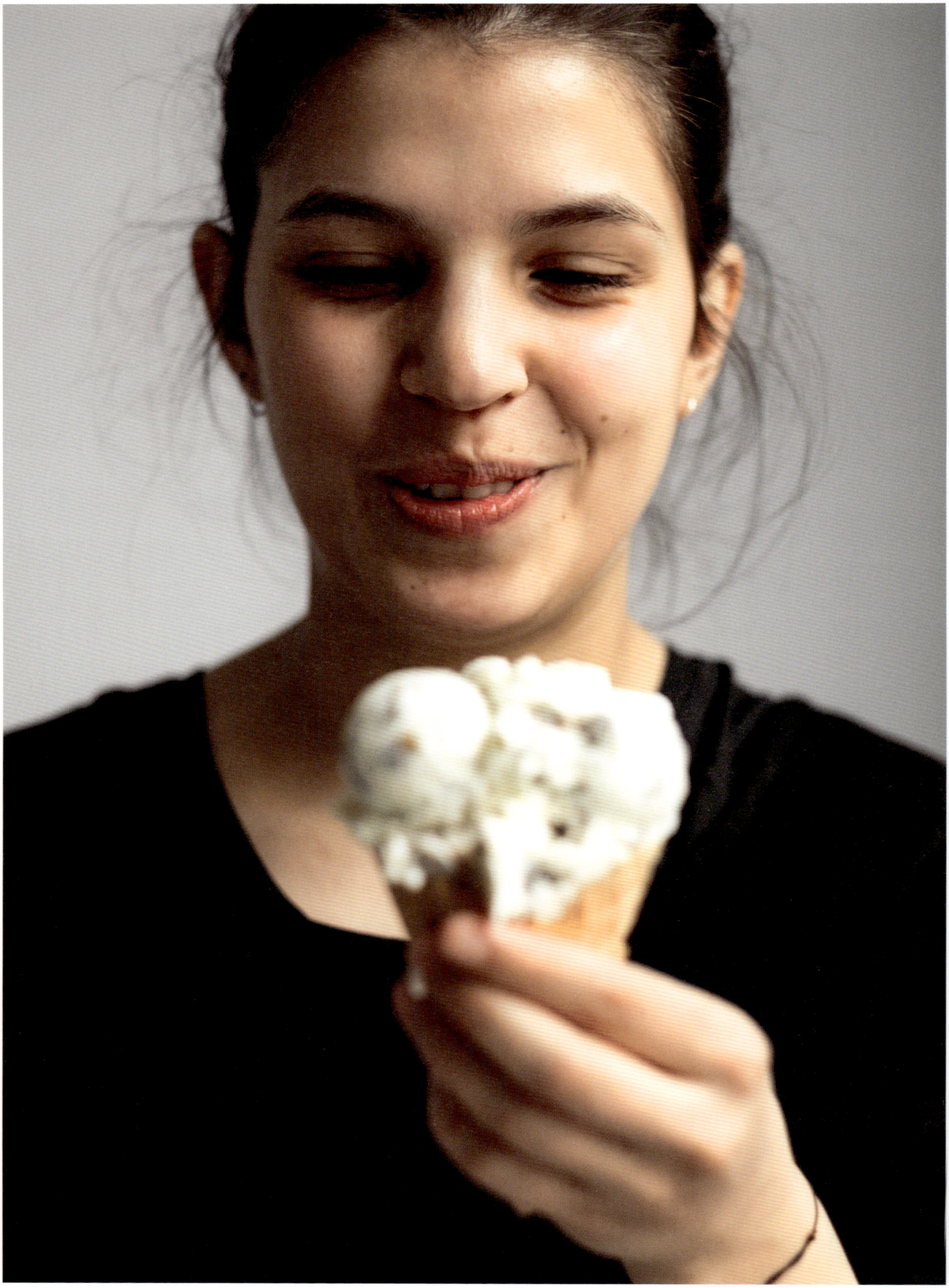

Nougat

The procedure here is straight forward – it is the timing of melting the sugar that can be tricky. Normally, hazelnuts are used for creating nougat. But thinking outside the box, here are no limitations to the ingredients you can add to the melted sugar, so I hope you will play around with it and make something fun. I have, on purpose, not given any suggestions for how much of the ingredient you should add. It is so individual what we like. So, time for trial and error.

100 g	sucrose
1 tsp	sea salt
+	various ingredients

PREPARATION The sucrose is melted on a heavy-bottomed pan until it is golden and completely dissolved (no sugar crystals left). You might have to stir in it once in a while to avoid burning, but be careful it does not clump together.

While you are waiting for this, prepare a piece of baking paper on a heat resistant surface. When all the sucrose is liquid, you add the sea salt and your ingredients. In this book I recommend you add nuts and dried flowers, but only your imagination is the limit. I do not, however, recommend adding something with a high water content as this will not go well with the crunchy nougat.

When the ingredients are stirred in, you pour the liquid nougat onto a baking paper and let it cool down. When completely hard, chop it up and store dry in an airtight container at room temperature.

TIP 1 If you are adding nuts, I prefer to roast them slightly in the oven first: 180°C for 8 minutes.

TIP 2 If you wish to store the ice cream with nougat in the freezer for a while, I recommend you coat the nougat pieces in a flavour neutral vegetable oil. This generates a coating, which makes it hard for the water in the ice cream to dissolve the crystalline sucrose from the nougat. Hence, the nougat will remain crunchy for a longer time.

Irish cream stracciatella

The notes of whiskey and spices go well together with the richness of an ice cream. Adding pieces of dark chocolate contributes with some bite and small hints of bitterness.

265 g	cream
215 g	skimmed milk
120 g	sucrose
70 g	skimmed milk powder
40 g	glucose
40 g	egg yolk
2 g	locust bean gum
250 g	Irish cream
100 g	chocolate

PREPARATION

Add all the ingredients, except the Irish cream, in a heavy-bottomed pot and heat up until it reaches 85°C whilst constantly stirring. If you want to have all the alcohol evaporate away, feel free to heat up the Irish cream together with the other ingredients.

Blend it really well, make an ice bath until the mix is 5°C, and leave to age in the fridge. This base is quite thick because 25% liquid is missing.

Blend the base together with the Irish cream and freeze. While freezing you can chop the chocolate. When the ice cream is scoopable, you add the chocolate by gently folding it in.

SCIENCE NOTES

The composition for this recipe is:

25% Irish cream, 16% total sugars, 10% dairy fat, 10% MSNF, 4% egg yolks, 0.2% locust bean gum

You might have noticed that this recipe is identical to the beer and espresso recipe. Now try the recipe with whatever you like.

Cookie dough

150 g	butter
70 g	sucrose
95 g	brown sugar
70 g	eggs, pasteurised (they will be consumed raw)
180 g	wheat flour
1 pinch	salt
115 g	dark chocolate
75 g	hazelnuts

PREPARATION

Whisk the butter, sucrose and brown sugar until the mix is creamy and smooth.

Whip in the eggs and then sift in the flour and salt. Mix it until everything is completely incorporated.

Chop the chocolate and slightly roast the nuts in the oven: 8 minutes at 180°C before chopping them, too.

Then add the chopped chocolate and chopped hazelnuts. Be careful not to over mix so the dough turns completely brown.

Place the cookie dough on a piece of baking paper and roll it into a log. Freeze down until you are using it, and then cut it into small pieces ready to put in the ice cream.

Take 1 kg of any base, add some vanilla, freeze and add the cookie dough pieces when the ice cream is scoopable.

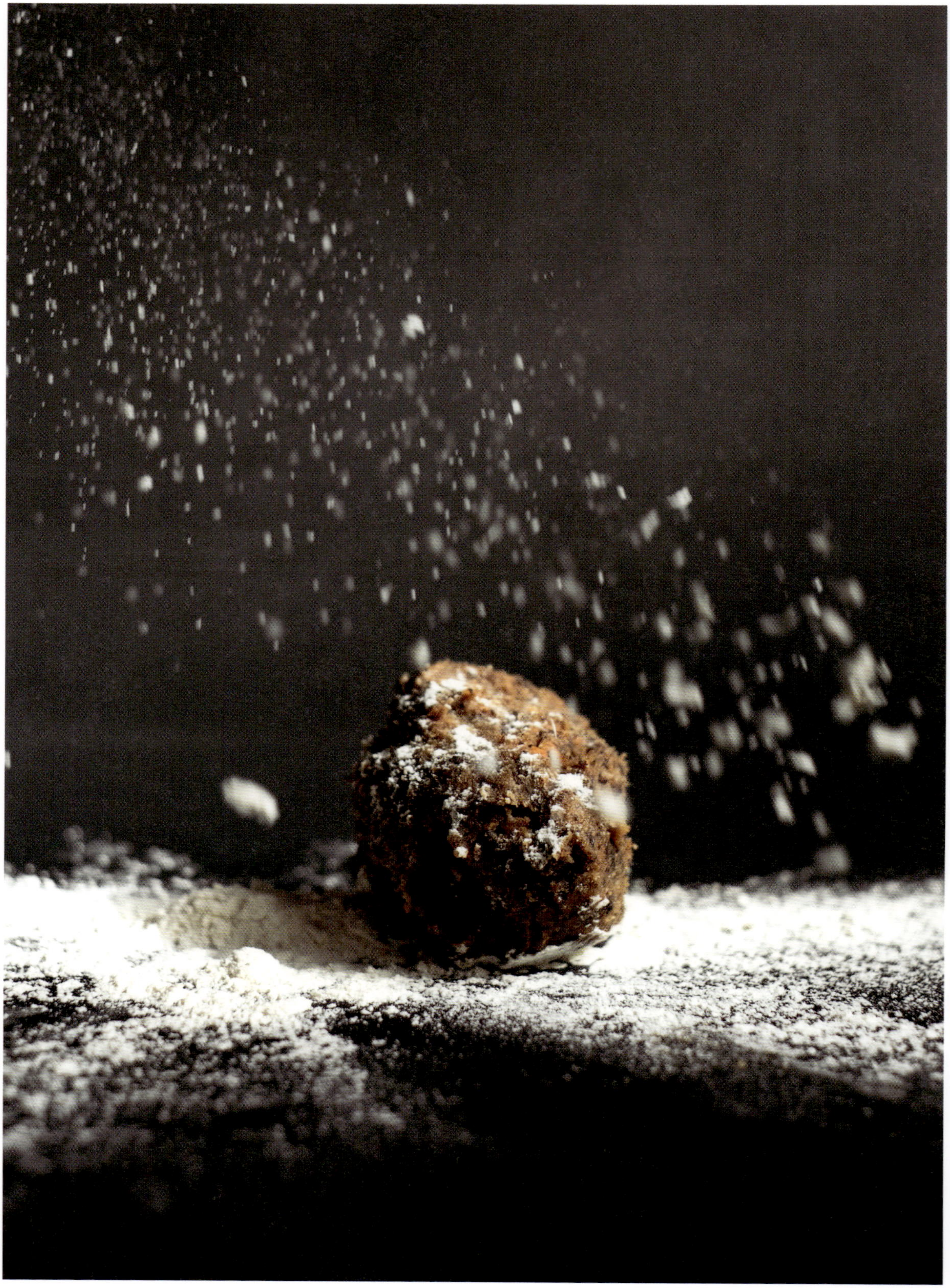

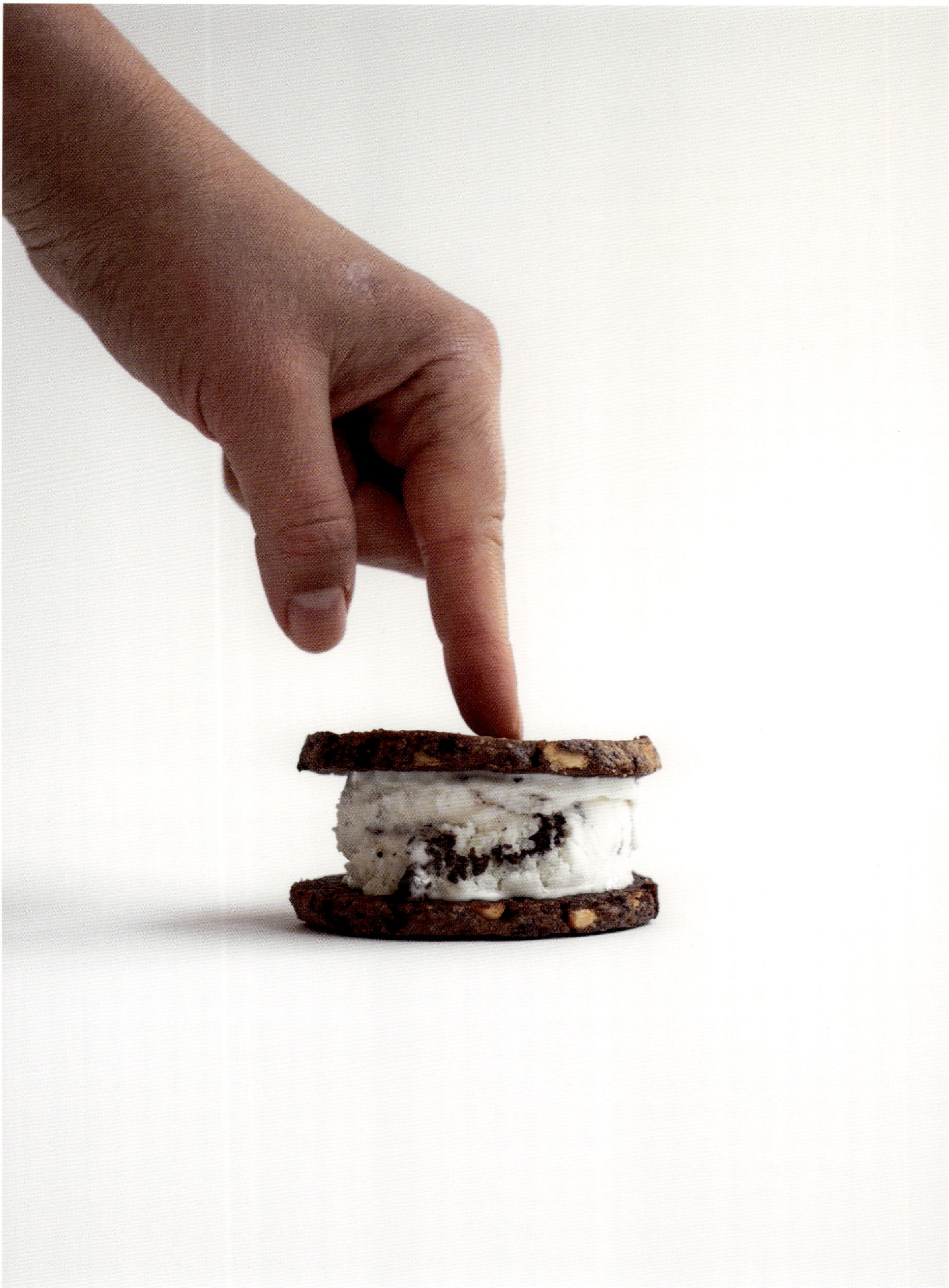

Cookies

The ideal ice cream cookie for making ice cream sandwiches should be crunchy, thin, not too sweet and relatively neutral flavoured. This makes it ideal for keeping focus on the ice cream and keeping the ice cream from being squeezed out between the two cookies.

You can also use sorbets, but usually sorbets are quite soft, so it can be hard to make sure they do not squeeze out too much between the two cookies. This recipe makes around 30 cookies depending on the size you make.

150 g	butter
115 g	sucrose
115 g	brown sugar
2	eggs
225 g	wheat flour
½ tsp	salt
1 tsp	baking powder
115 g	dark chocolate
115 g	hazelnuts

PREPARATION **THE RIGHT WAY**

1. Whisk the butter, sucrose and brown sugar until smooth.

2. Add one egg at a time and whisk until everything is combined.

3. Sift in the flour, salt and baking powder and mix it until completely incorporated.

4. Chop the chocolate and roast the hazelnuts in a 180°C oven for 8 minutes. and chop them too. Add the chocolate and hazelnuts to the dough and then leave for 30 minutes in the fridge.

5. Add a chunk of the cookie dough between two pieces of baking paper and roll it flat until it is 2–3 mm thick. Put it on a baking tray and then leave it in the fridge for another 15 minutes. Do this with all the cookie dough.

6. Take it out from the fridge and then cut the cookie dough with a round cookie cutter. Alternatively, you can use a glass with sharp edges. Remove the dough around the cookie cutter, save it all, and roll it out between two pieces of parchment paper again.

7. Bake the cookies in a pre-heated oven at 180°C for about 10 minutes or until the cookies are golden brown on the edges.

8. Leave the cookies to cool down on a wire rack. When completely cold, you can scoop your preferred ice cream onto one cookie and top it with another cookie. Alternatively, you can store the cookies in an airtight container for another day.

PREPARATION **THE FAST WAY**

Mix all the ingredients together and continue from step 5.

Nut paste

Use it for your nut flavoured ice creams or just spread it on bread – it tastes fantastic! I recommend making a big batch and storing it in the fridge. The shelf life is good for a couple of weeks. Put it in the fridge if you want to avoid oxidation and rancid, potent flavours.

300 g   nuts (pistachio, hazelnuts, cashew nuts, walnuts, pecan nuts…)

PREPARATION

Fill up a baking tray with unroasted and unsalted nuts without shells. Bake the nuts for approximately 30 minutes in a pre-heated 150°C convection oven. Take them out and taste them. If they have a very dark roasted flavour they are done. It should be so dark roasted that you almost do not want to consume them. This brings out the flavour really well in the ice cream.

While the nuts are still warm, blend them thoroughly in a food processor until they become liquid. If this seems impossible, you can add 1–2 tsp vegetable oil (flavour neutral) and it will become liquid. The nut paste is now ready to use.

To make the nut ice creams, I always recommend using base 3, variety A, since the dextrose lowers the freezing point further. This is needed because there is a high amount of fat in nuts, which generates a harder ice cream.

For all the nut ice creams, you can add a nougat made with the same nuts. It gives some crunch and complexity to the clean nut flavour.

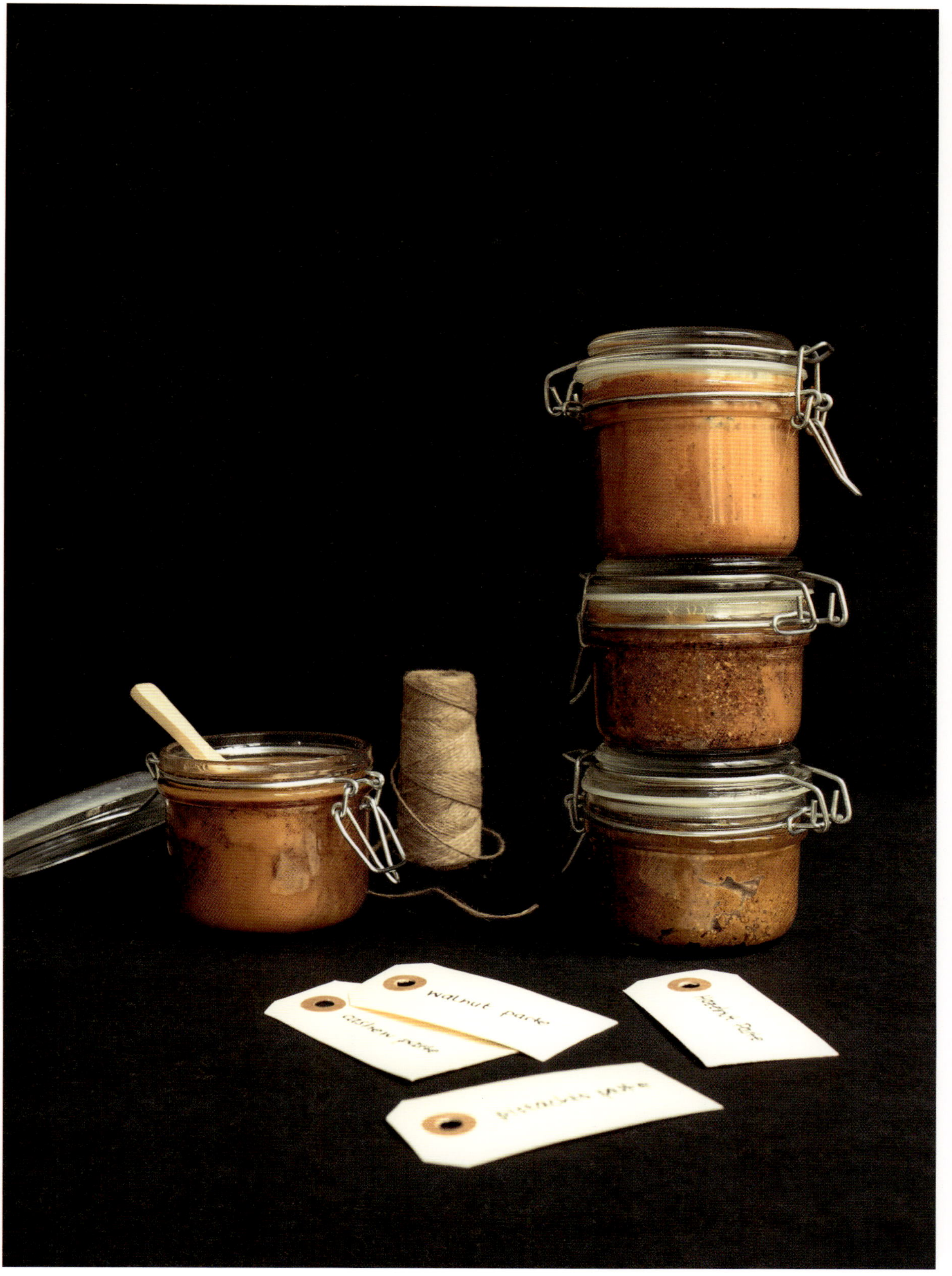
walnut paste
cashew paste

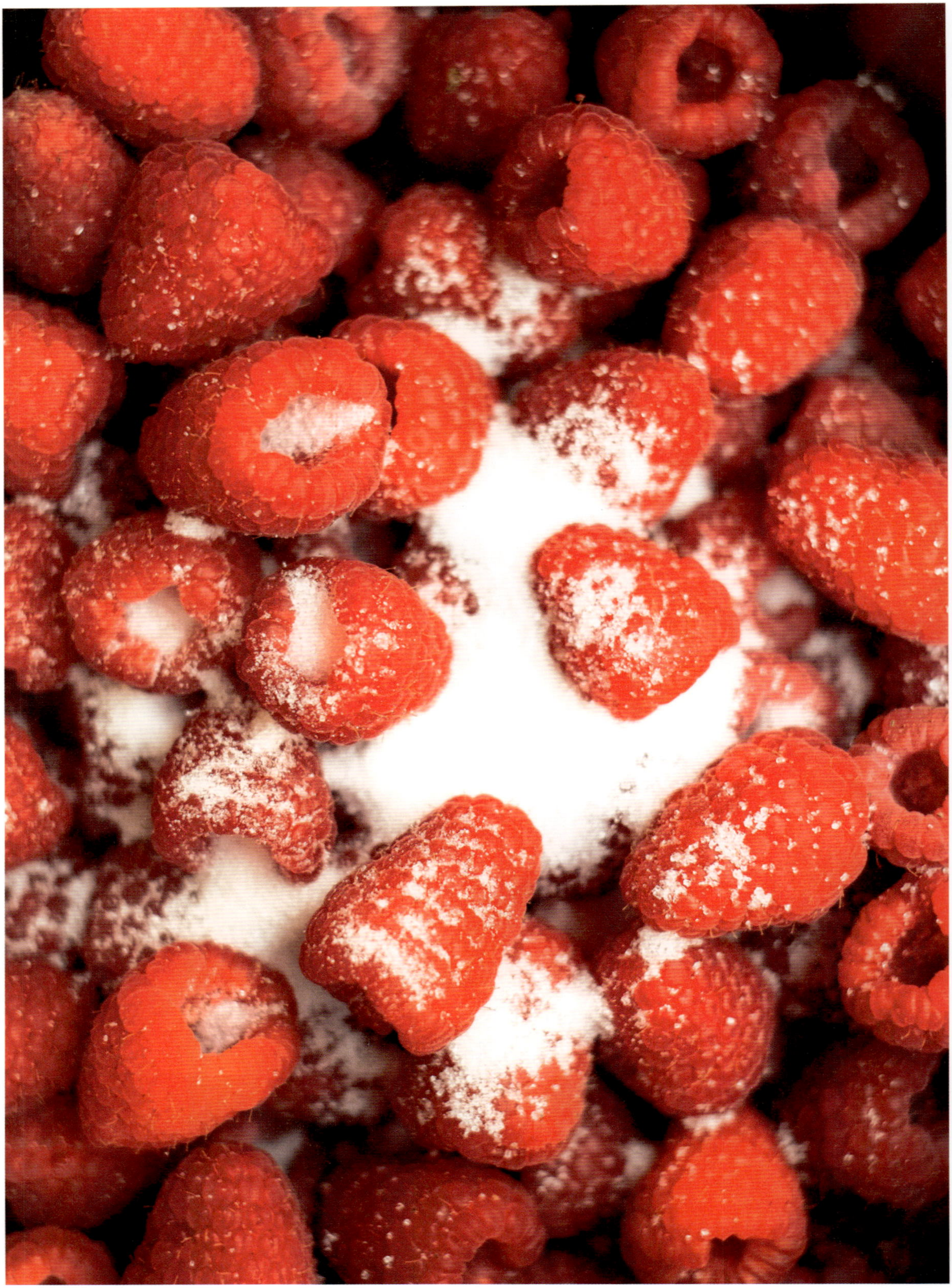

Fruit sauce

A good fruit sauce for ice cream needs to contain around 50% sugars in order not to be icy when frozen down (FPDF matters here too). The below recipe is valid for most fruits, but you might have to add some lemon juice to get the acidity right.

500 g	fruit
300 g	sucrose
200 g	glucose

PREPARATION Boil all the ingredients together and blend. Cool down in the fridge and add it to the ice cream when it is refrigerated. If it is too warm it will melt the ice cream and create ice crystals.

If you want to make for instance a sauce from fruit juice, I recommend you to add 2–3 g locust bean gum to the above recipe in order to thicken the sauce a little bit. Most berries contain fibres and some pectin, which will help thicken it.

Cones

And what is ice cream without a cone? Especially now-a-days where everyone is talking about sustainability. Cones are biodegradable with no waste. And they taste amazing.

So if you can get your hands on a waffle iron and a cone mould, it is worth making these from scratch.

60 g	butter
100 g	egg whites
65 g	wheat flour
60 g	sucrose

PREPARATION Melt the butter, and blend all the ingredients together and pour 2–3 tablespoons onto the preheated waffle iron (I am not talking about a Belgian waffle iron which makes soft and mooshy waffles). Once done, fold the cone around a cone mould and let sit for a few seconds to harden.

You can experiment with adding vanilla, almond, tonka beans, coffee or something else to your cones to add some flavour.

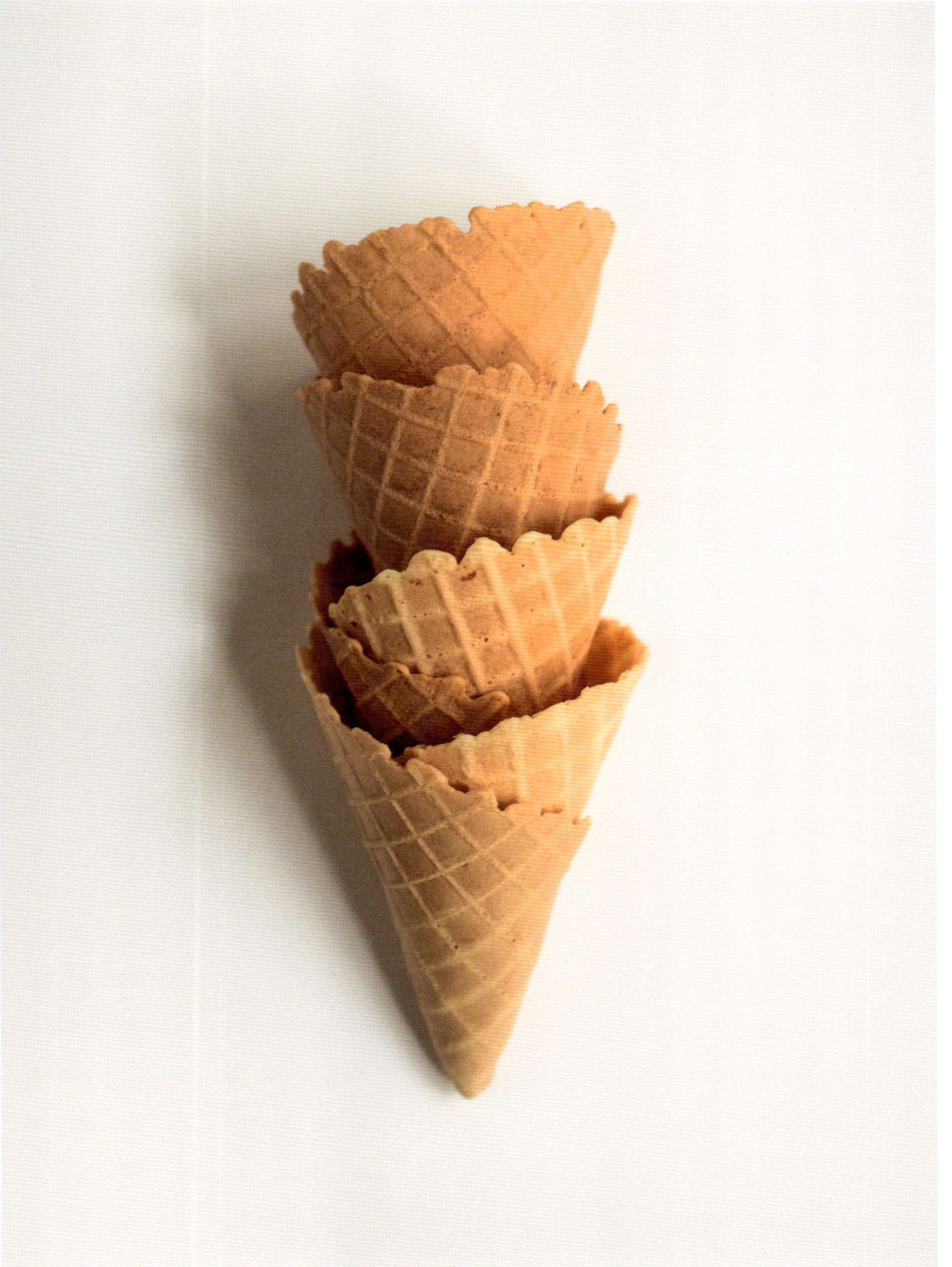

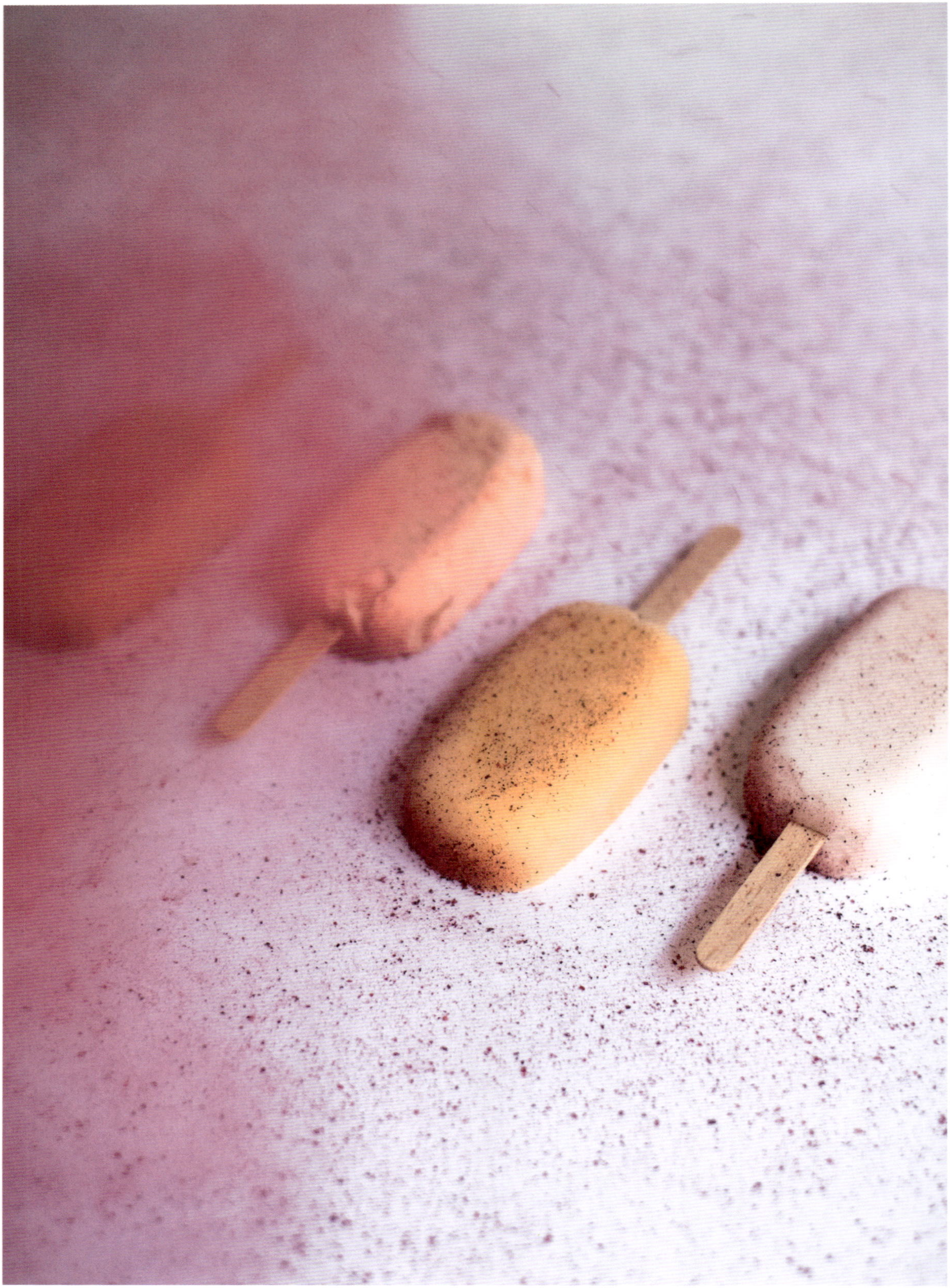

Sticks

PREPARATION Produce your favourite ice cream or sorbet and make it a bit harder by following base 3, variety B or syrup 3, variety B. We want the sticks to be hard enough so we can get them out of the moulds, so be careful with ice creams and sorbets that contain sugars with high FPDF or alcohol.

Freeze the ice cream or sorbet in the machine and fill the stick moulds straight after. Keep the moulds in the freezer so they are cold when you are filling them. Put them into the storage freezer immediately and leave them overnight. Just remember to put the sticks in – if you forget and they are hard it is really difficult – I speak from experience.

If you wish to decorate the sticks with melted chocolate, prepare this just before you are ready to take the sticks out of the freezer.

Place a piece of baking paper on a tray or a cutting board, and gently take the sticks out of the moulds and place them on the baking paper. Either you drizzle the melted chocolate with a spoon over the sticks or you dip one stick at a time in the hot chocolate and place it back on the baking paper. If you want to sprinkle nuts/flakes over the sticks, you have to be fast before the chocolate is hardened. Put the sticks back in the freezer for a minimum of one hour.

Melting chocolate

PREPARATION

This is the section where I could describe a lot about tempering the chocolate properly and warnings if you do not do it and so on. The chocolate is frozen down, so it will get 'the crack' even if it is not tempered.

If you are super-skilled in this field, be my guest, and temper your chocolate. Personally, I do not because there is not much difference after freezing down anyway. You can use either white, dark or milk chocolate for this.

Melt the chocolate in a bowl on top of a pot with warm water until the chocolate is liquid. Add it to a tall glass, which is surrounded by very warm water to keep the chocolate warm. Dipping the sticks in the hot chocolate will lower the temperature of the chocolate, so it can be hard to keep coating the sticks if you do not make sure the chocolate keeps warm.

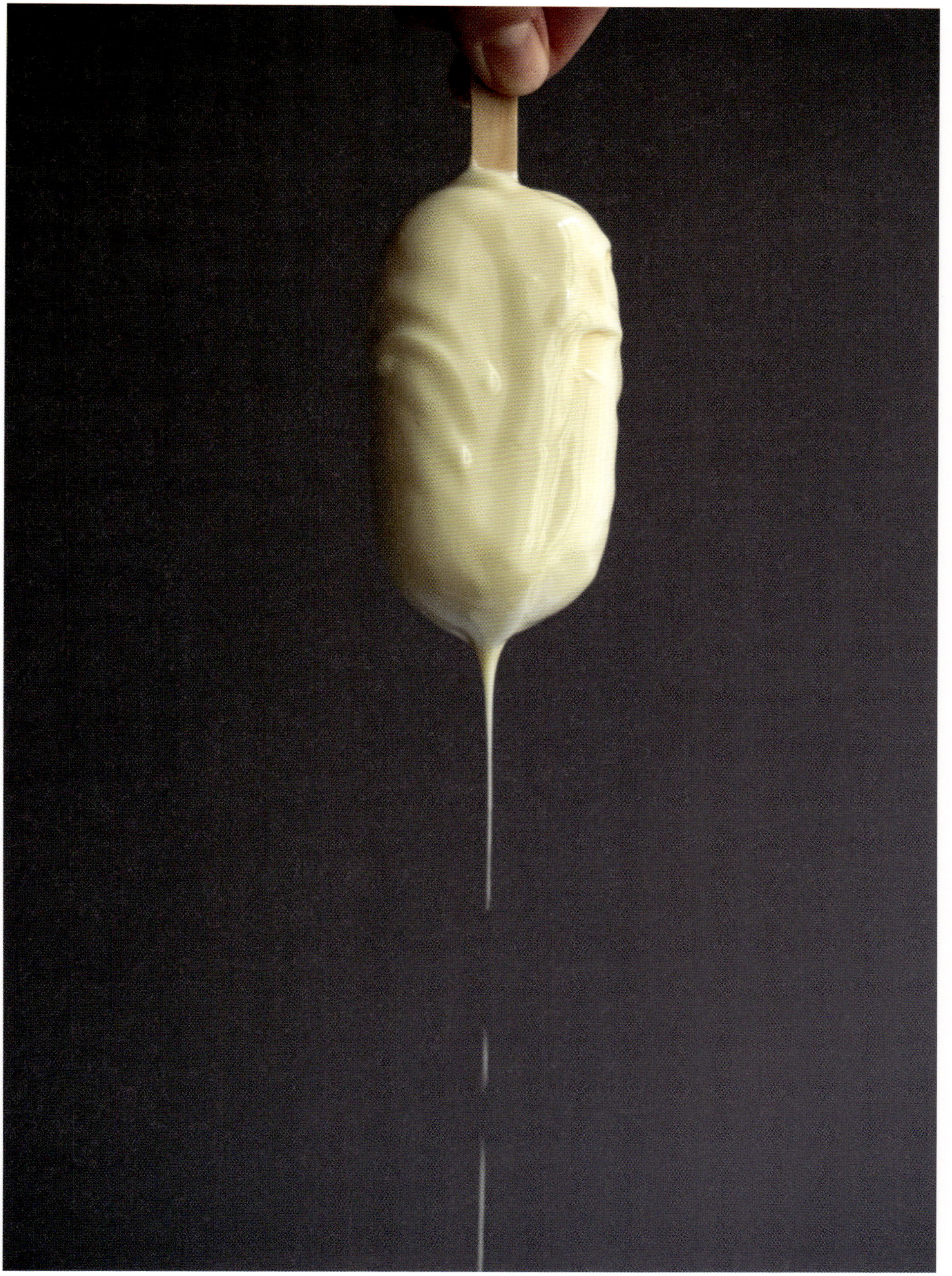

Cakes

PREPARATION

1. Choose three ice cream or sorbet flavours; one is the outer layer and you need 1 litre of this. The other two will be inside and you need 0.75 litres of each (give or take depending on your pan size).

2. Prepare an adjustable, round cake pan (Ø18–22 cm) by placing a piece of baking paper in the bottom. Put it in the freezer for 20 minutes.

3. Scoop the flavour for the outer layer into the pan and press it down gently with a spoon and up on the sides so it is around 1 cm thick. Make sure to press it very flat so there are no air gaps. Put the cake back in the freezer for 30 minutes or more.

4. Add the second layer by scooping it in and flattening it with a spoon. It should make up around half of the remaining part in the pan. Put the cake back in the freezer for minimum 30 minutes.

5. Add the third layer by scooping it in and flattening it with a spoon until it is levelled with the first outer layer. Put the cake back in the freezer for a minimum of 4 hours.

6. Take out the pan and wet a cloth with warm water. Rub the cloth around the sides of the mould and keep adding more hot water to the cloth as needed. Be careful not to get any water onto the cake or this will create ice crystals.

7. When the mould can release from the sides, take it out, and with a spatula flatten the sides so there are no air gaps and it has a nice finish. Flip the cake upside down onto a cake tray. It is a good idea to keep this tray in the freezer to make sure the cake does not melt on it.

8. Flatten the top of the cake with a spatula and then decorate it with whatever you wish. I prefer a fine pattern with melted chocolate.

TIP 1 If you want to add a bottom, bake the brownie from page 94 and cut it out in a size 2–3 cm smaller in diameter than the actual cake mould so it fits inside the outer layer of ice cream.

TIP 2 It is a good idea to have a strong structured ice cream/sorbet in the bottom layer because it has to carry the weight of cutting through the cake. The middle layer can be a bit softer and the outer layer has to have a good meltdown stability, because it has a big surface area exposed to the warm air and is therefore more prone to melt.

TIP 3 Cut the cake with a very sharp knife as this gives the best cut.

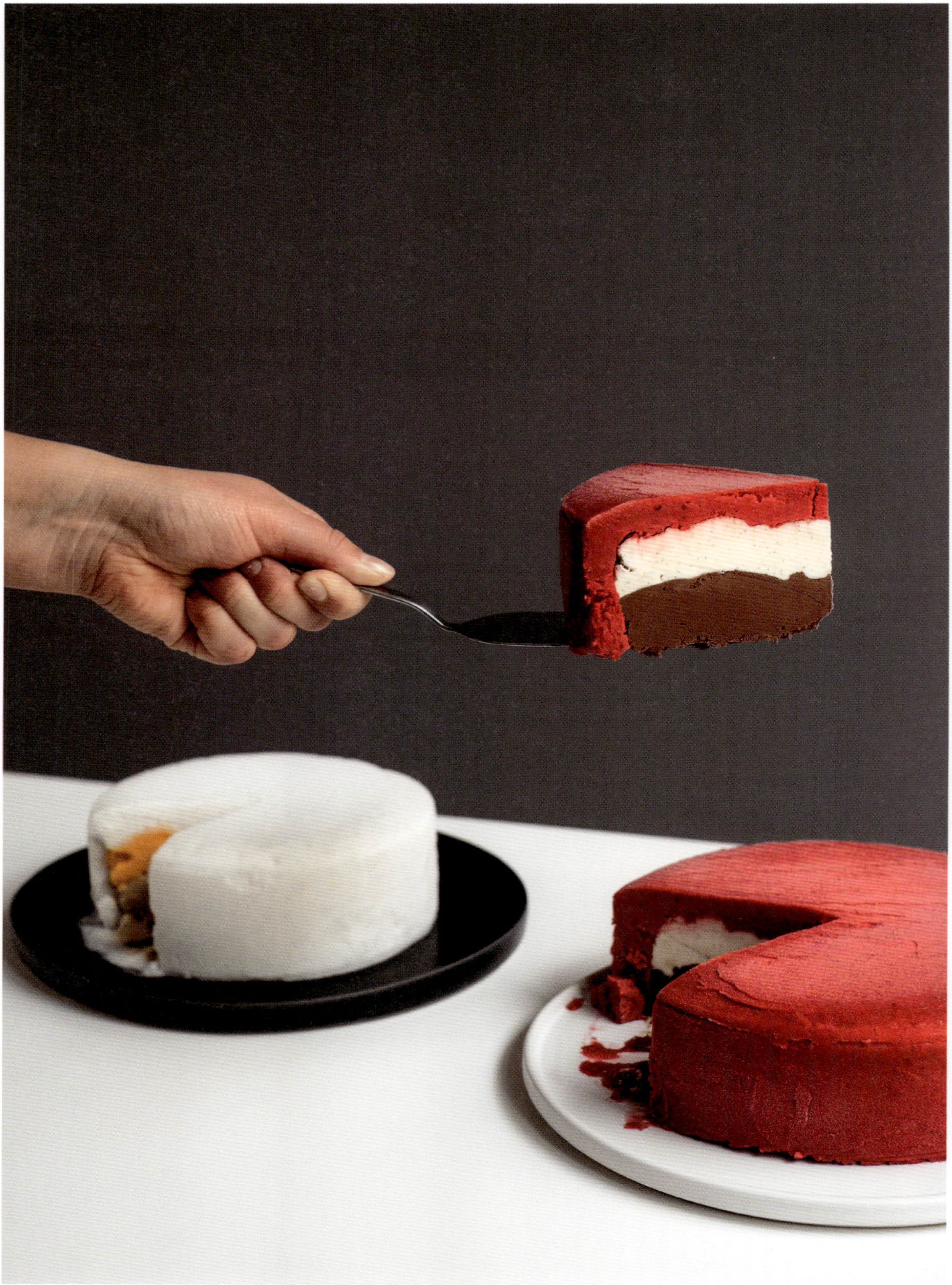

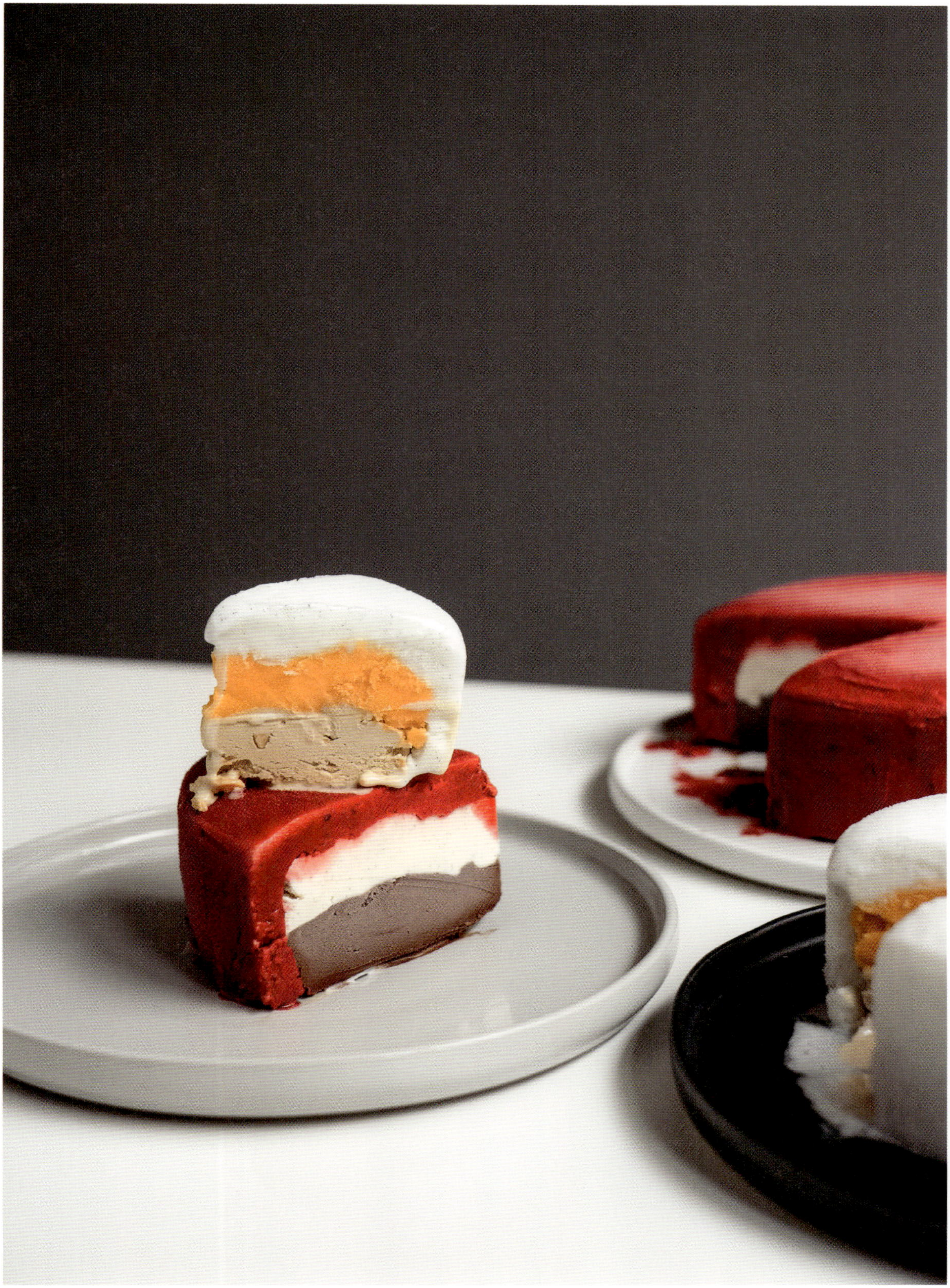

SCIENCE

Now it is time to go through some of the fundamentals when working with ice cream. Please get ready to dive into the magical world of ice cream science.

- Cream
- Milk
- Egg
- Sucrose
- Glucose
- Dextrose
- Skimmed milk power
- Locust bean gum

Ingredients

"Why is this added?" or "what is this?" you might have asked yourself as you have read through the recipes. For you to really understand everything in depth, I have provided some information on how to choose your ingredients and combining them in the best way. I have chosen the most commonly used ingredients for making ice cream and sorbet and this will give you a simple outline of their composition and functionalities.

MILK

There are several types of milk available, and whether you decide to use skimmed milk, low- fat milk or whole milk, it does not really matter when calculating recipes. As long as the composition of the specific type of milk is known and accounted for in the calculations.

Skimmed milk is the simplest milk to use for this purpose, because we can pretend it has a fat content of 0%. This means that we can break down skimmed milk into only two components: water and Milk Solids Non-Fat (MSNF). It might sound weird that milk contains water, but I want you to know that almost all our food contains water, whether it is bread, vegetables, meat, or dairy products.

MSNF is a term that covers all the milk solids that are not fat, being: milk proteins (whey and casein), milk sugar (lactose), minerals, vitamins, acids and enzymes.

Per definition, skimmed milk contains 9% MSNF and the remaining 91% is water.

Once you know the fat% of a milk or cream, you can calculate the MSNF content from below, because the remaining part of a milk/cream after subtracting the fat% is skimmed milk.

(Eq. 1) $\quad\%MSNF = (100 - fat\%) \times 0.09$

If we for instance use whole milk (3.5% fat), the remaining part (96.5%) of the whole milk is therefore skimmed milk. This equals to 8.7% MSNF in the whole milk as can be seen from inserting the values in equation 1:

$$\% MSNF_{whole\ milk} = (100 - 3.5) \times 0.09 = 8.7\%$$

CREAM

Cream is a good source of dairy fat, which is essential for making ice cream. The fat content may vary depending on the brand of the cream and country it is sold in. This book uses cream with a fat content of 38%, as this is most commonly found in Denmark. From the above equation 1, we can easily calculate the MSNF composition of cream:

Knowing 38% is fat, the remaining 62% is skimmed milk. From this we can calculate a content of 5.6% MSNF in our cream:

$$\% \text{ MSNF}_{cream} = (100 - 38\%) \times 0.09 = 5.6\%$$

Dairy fat is very unique in its composition because of its content of both liquid and solid fat at frozen temperatures. The ratio of these fatty acids makes dairy fat ideal for developing a strong fat structure in the ice cream. Preferably, there should be many small fat globules in the ice cream base, so starting out with a cream that has been homogenised helps us a long way. More about this is under the paragraphs on homogenisation and structure.

MILK POWDER

Ice cream needs to contain proteins as these play a role in incorporating air, emulsifying the fat and making an ice cream more viscous and full-bodied in texture. Milk powders are a good source of proteins.

If you evaporate off all the water in a certain type of milk, you end up with milk powder. Milk powder is therefore a very concentrated form of MSNF hereunder milk proteins and milk sugar.

In theory, you can either choose to cook your milk for a very long time yourself at home until it is a powder*, or you can buy it ready made. I strongly recommend that you buy it – it will save you a lot time and you can avoid burning your best pots and pans.

---

* Ok, this does not really happen because we start seeing Maillard reactions, which creates a caramel before we actually get to the powder stage. In theory you would need some special equipment to make your own powder. So please do not try this at home.

To keep things simple, I choose skimmed milk powder to keep the sources of fat to a minimum in the recipe calculations.

In table 1 the compositional information of the most commonly used dairy products is gathered.

TABLE 1. Compositional information of various dairy products needed to calculate base recipes.

Ingredient	Fat content	MSNF*	Water**
Skimmed milk	0-0.1%	9%	91%
Whole milk	3.5 %	8.7%*	87.8%
Cream (35%)	35 %	5.9%*	59.1%
Cream (38%)	38%	5.6%*	56.4%
Skimmed milk powder	0%	97%	2-3%

* Values are calculated from Equation 1. MSNF: Milk Solids Non-Fat
** 100% - fat% - MSNF%

SUGARS

Understanding your sugar science is so important I decided to allocate a chapter on this below. For now, you just need to know the following: Besides being a sweetener, sugar also helps with making ice creams and sorbets nice and soft because they depress the freezing point.

The term "sugar" covers a wide variety of different kinds of sugars. What we normally refer to as "sugar" has the chemical nomenclature sucrose or saccharose. I have used the term "sucrose" throughout the book to avoid confusion with other kinds of sugar.

Other sugars often used are glucose and dextrose (and fructose you might come across). And of course, the lactose which is present in the MSNF fraction of milk, cream and milk powders. The main structural ingredients in sorbets are sugars of different kinds, so choosing the right sugars for the right recipes is essential for creating a soft and not-too-sweet product.*

If you see a sugar which is liquid, I want you to think water. For instance, a liquid glucose contains water and is often only 70–80% actual glucose. If you want to be very specific you need to remember to calculate the actual amount of solid sugars, if you are using liquid sugars. On page 135 we will go into more details about the different kinds of sugars and how they affect the ice cream and sorbet.

EMULSIFIERS An emulsifier is a compound that can bind two phases that do not like to mix. In ice cream this is fat and water. From reading about milk and cream, I hope you now know that there is water in both of these.

An emulsifier can be something as natural as egg yolks and to a certain extent, milk proteins. Egg yolks contain phospholipids and lipoproteins, which have amphiphilic properties, meaning they can bind to both fat and water.

A suggested level of egg yolks, for optimal emulsifying properties, in ice cream is around 2–4%. Trust me, I wrote a long thesis on this topic, but I will save you the details and just share the results. We want to emulsify our ice cream base because it allows the fat to destabilize and partially coalesce, creating a network that is great at stabilising air. On page 24 you can see the effect egg yolks have on the air incorporation of an ice cream.

If you use whole eggs, it can be beneficial to know that approximately 1/3 (~20 g) of a whole egg is egg yolk and 2/3 (~40 g) is egg white, so we need to use three times as much whole eggs as egg yolks in order to get the same emulsifying properties. Totally, a whole egg contains 75% water and the rest are solids: protein, fat and a small amount of carbohydrates.

---

* The food industry has made things a bit confusing, because dextrose is actually glucose, and glucose is sometimes called corn syrup solids. Glucose is hydrolysed from a starch, maltodextrin, and glucose is often followed by the term "dextrose equivalent" (DE) in order to explain how hydrolysed the glucose syrup is. This is a bit of a longer explanation, and in order not to get too confused, we stick with the terms the food industry has created and this is what you can buy in the stores.

In the absence of egg yolks or other small molecular emulsifiers, milk proteins will act as an emulsifier because these proteins also have different parts that can bind to both fat and water. The proteins will interact with the fat, but the result will not be the same as when smaller molecular compounds are used. Read more under "structure", page 130).

Industrially, it is quite common to use some very small molecular emulsifiers such as mono- and diglycerides. They are extremely efficient at building a strong network and they do not contribute with flavour or colour to the ice cream like egg yolks do. So next time you read the back of an ice cream container you will know what these do.

FIBRES Fibres can be a good source of additional solids in ice cream and sorbet. For instance, this is a key component when trying to keep the sugar content low or when trying to increase viscosity by binding water. Fibres can be present by using fruits and vegetables. The fibres can also be added in its pure form, for instance as inulin. It is unfortunately beyond the scope of this book to cover fibres in much more detail. But as you will learn, after making a lot of recipes, using whole fruits like avocadoes, bananas, berries and so on help make the sorbets smoother and creamier than for instance just using fruit juices.

STABILISERS A very commonly used group of stabilisers in ice cream and sorbet are gums derived from plants and trees such as guar gum and locust bean gum. The advantage of using gums lies in their water binding capacity, which helps increase the viscosity of the water phase. Increasing the viscosity gives a more full-bodied ice cream structure and it inhibits ice crystal growth during temperature fluctuations.

I want to clear a common misunderstanding: stabilisers have little to do with how an ice cream or sorbet melts. Stabilisers help stabilise the water, ice and sugar phase whereas the role of fat, emulsifiers and air is much more important for the meltdown, hence the level and type of emulsifier needs to be carefully selected.

It is getting more and more common to source a blend of stabilisers for use in small household productions. Depending on the kinds of stabiliser used and whether the blend also contains an emulsifier, a recommended dosage would be around 0.4–0.6%. Certain stabilisers can have a synergistic effect on each other, but if you use only one kind of plant derived stabiliser, you do not need to add a lot more than 0.1–0.3%. If you add more, the ice cream or sorbet can get unpleasantly sticky and gummy. And make sure to read up on how the stabiliser is affected by temperatures. Some stabilisers need higher mixing temperatures to increase the water binding capacity.

AIR Air deserves attention since it is such an important part of a creamy ice cream and sorbet. Sometimes ice cream manufacturers proudly tell me, that there is no air in their ice cream. I respond as politely as I can, saying that "I am pretty sure there is, otherwise it would be a very hard chunk of ice. But I assume you are just not pumping any air into it under pressure".

When producing ice cream on small household machines (and batch freezers for that matter), we cannot really control the air content but trust me when I say that it is incorporated. To what extent depends on how the recipe has been formulated and prepared, and how long the ice cream is being whipped and frozen in the ice cream machine. During the freezing cycle, it is especially fat and protein that help stabilise the air bubbles.

Air bubbles help make an ice cream smooth, and air is a good insulator and makes sure the ice cream and sorbet do not feel too cold in the mouth.

Colour wise, we also need to consider what air does to the final product. The colour is always more intense in the unfrozen mix when there is no air incorporated that will inevitably dilute the colour intensity. So, if you are playing around with colours in your ice cream, you need to make them much more intense in the mix than you actually want in your frozen and aerated product.

The air content varies a lot from different ice cream brands and types. In these recipes there will typically be 20–30% air if you add egg yolks or egg whites. On page 24 you can see how the addition of egg yolks and egg whites influence the air incorporation.

In some commercial brands you can get up to 50% air or more. So, unless you want to buy a lot of air it can be beneficial to check how heavy your 1 litre of ice cream actually is.

COMPOSITION The composition of an ice cream and sorbet is important if we want a rich and creamy texture. For sorbets it is quite simple: make sure there is around 20-30% sugars present in the final product and the rest is water and maybe some stabiliser and egg whites.

However, when it comes to ice cream, there are many factors that need to be considered.

Finding a balance in the amount of total solids, fat and MSNF is important. A high total solids content will result in a high viscosity, which will inhibit air incorporation because it is too heavy. Too low solids content will give a very thin mouth feeling and also little air incorporation because there is not enough protein and fat to stabilize the air bubbles. The "right" amount will enable a good air content and strong mouth feeling – i.e. the ice cream is richer and denser in texture. Below are some levels of the various components that are within a range where it cannot go completely wrong.

It is beyond the scope of this book to go much more into details with this, but hopefully you understand the "science notes" better now.

TABLE 2. Commonly used range of ice cream composition.

Component	Commonly used range
Fat	5-20%
Sugar	10-20%
MSNF	8-12%
Emulsifiers	2-4% (if egg yolks are used)
Stabilisers	0.1-0.3%

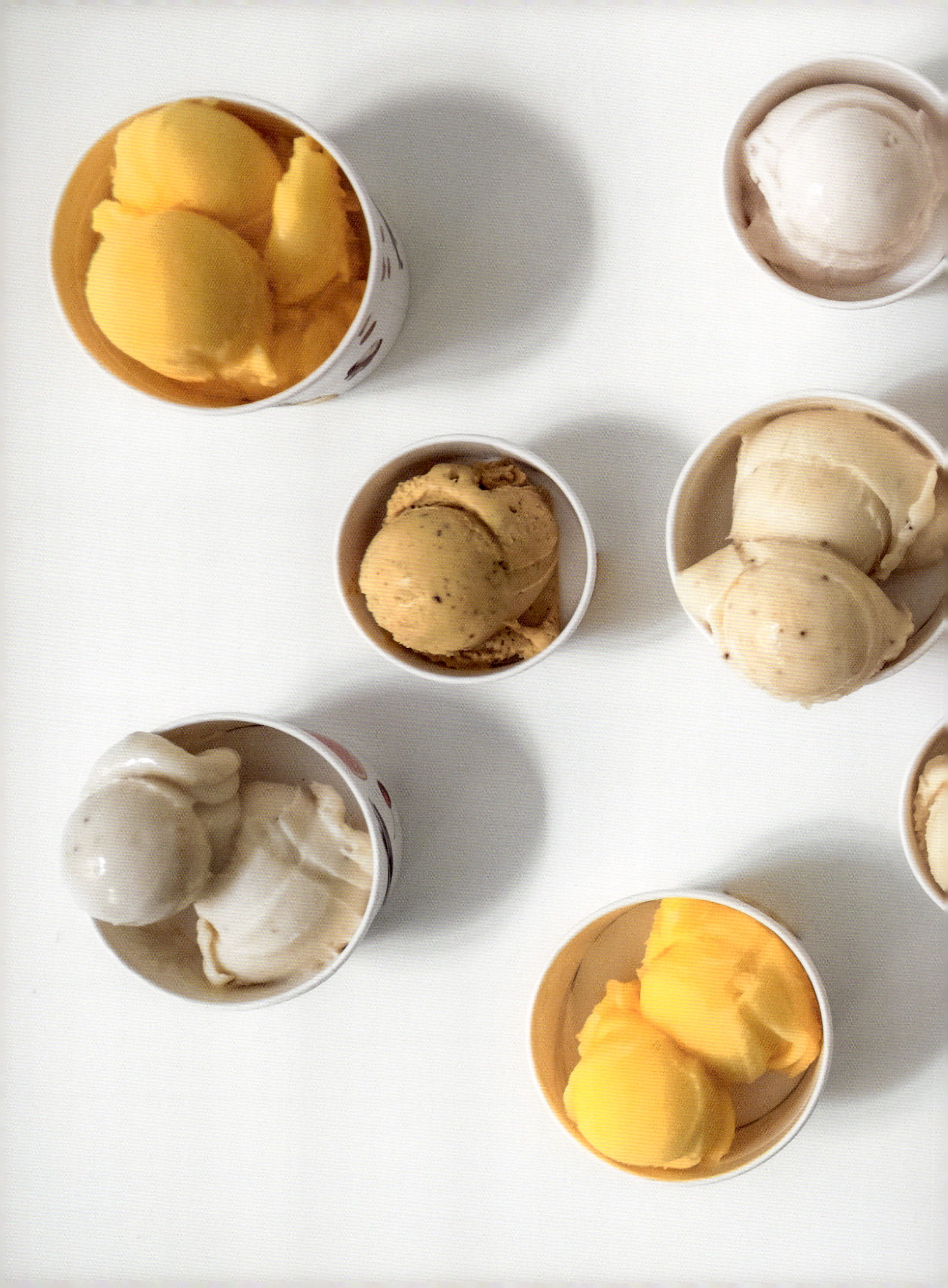

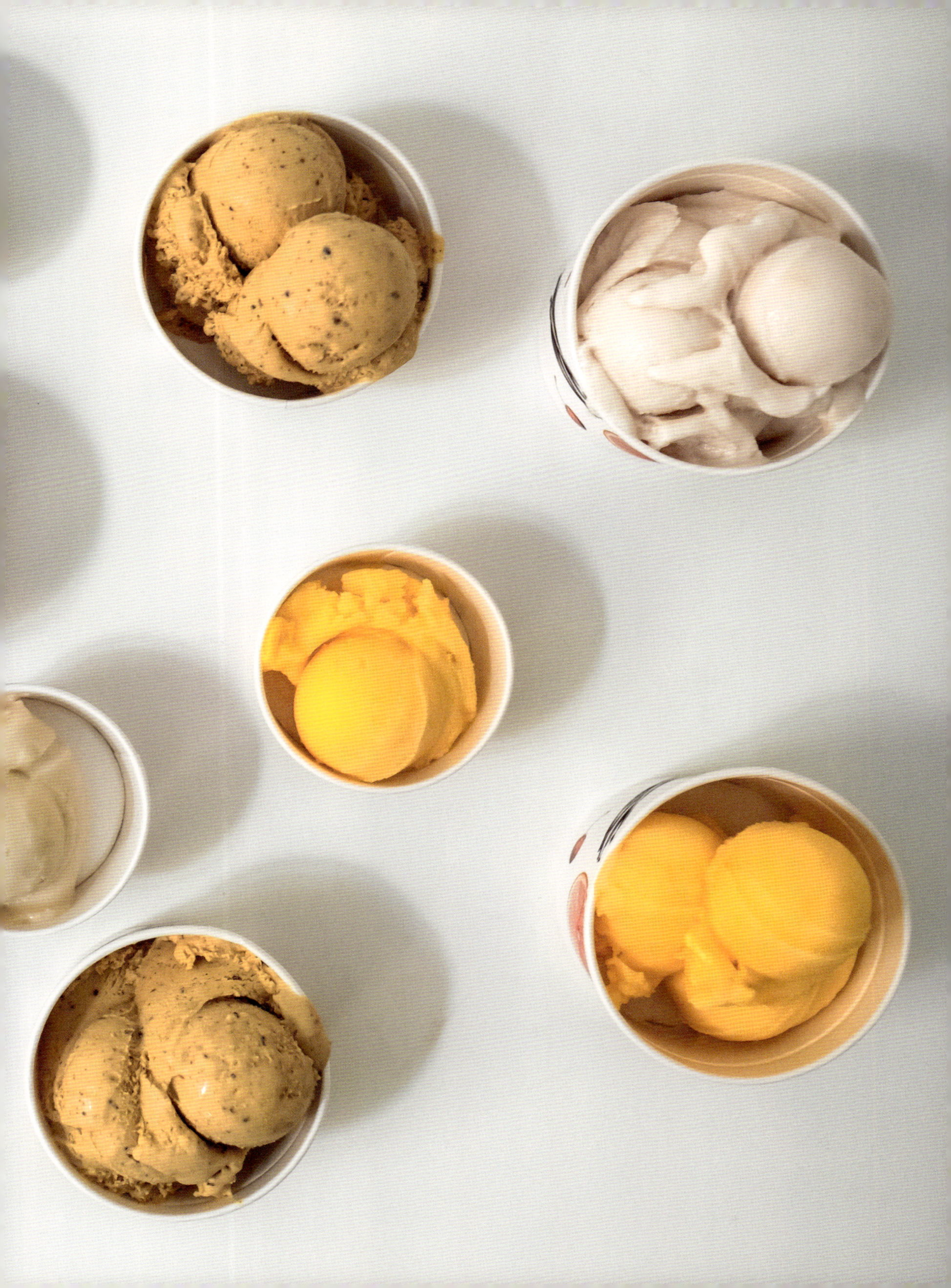

Production

Now that we know a bit about the different ingredients and components, it is time to get a better understanding of how the components work together during the different production steps, hereby creating a structure.

FORMULATING RECIPES is the part that requires knowledge, decision-making and science. Hence, this theoretical part of the book.

WEIGHING OFF your ingredients and mixing together is not hard. I just advise you to use scales, as this is the most precise method (and to make sure you reset them to zero with every new ingredient – we have all been guilty forgetting this...!).

PASTEURISATION, also called heat treatment, is necessary for several reasons: destruction of pathogenic bacteria so no one gets ill, denaturing some proteins, dissolving ingredients, melting milk fat and hydrating proteins/stabilisers.

HOMOGENISATION is important for breaking down larger fat globules into smaller fat globules. Optimally, you want to homogenise your warm mix. This means forcing your mix through a small orifice under high pressure. The majority of us do not have access to homogenisers, instead we can mimic this step by blending the warm mix thoroughly. Just to make life easier for our ice cream structure, it is a good idea to use cream that already has been homogenised. The step is also recommended for sorbet syrup, but mainly to make sure the syrup is homogenous.

AGEING is a step that is often neglected. Until now! This step is emphasised several places in this book, and if you should learn one thing from reading this book, it should be this. At this step you put your ice cream base or sorbet syrup in the fridge for at least 4 hours, but preferably overnight. It is a good idea to use an ice bath to cool it down so it is already 4–5°C when it is put in the fridge. This step is essential for generating a stable and airy ice cream structure and a thick sorbet syrup, which you will hopefully understand very soon.

INGREDIENTS ARE ADDED after the ageing process. This is the creative process, where you have to adjust the recipes to your personal preferences and play around with ingredients. This is also the time to taste the mix. Because if you wish to change something you can do it now. Once the mix has been frozen, there is not really any way back.

FREEZING AND WHIPPING are done together in ice cream machines with this general rule: the faster the freezing, the smoother the ice cream (fast freezing promotes the formation of more nuclei, hence many small ice crystals instead of fewer big crystals). However, a longer time in the ice cream machine can promote more air incorporation due to a longer whipping time.

It can be very difficult to freeze the ice cream fast enough in a household machine, since it usually freezes around 1.5 L in 20–40 min, depending on the machine. That is a relatively long time compared to a batch freezer, which can freeze 10–20 L in around 6–8 minutes. Industrially, ice cream can be frozen on continuous freezers within 30–60 seconds resulting in a very smooth structure. However, the longer freezing and whipping time can be good for incorporating air. But try to be fast in the freezing process and put your ice cream machine in cold surroundings to speed up the process.

INCLUSIONS ARE ADDED after the freezing and whipping step. You want to make sure the pieces and sauces are as cold as possible, so they do not melt any of the ice cream. The ice cream is usually quite soft at this stage and only around -5°C to -7°C, and that means the structure is fragile, so you need to work fast and get the ice cream in the freezer as quickly as possible.

HARDENING is done immediately after freezing and whipping or adding inclusions if you want to store your ice cream for another day. This more or less means freezing your ice cream as fast as possible to avoid growth of bigger ice crystals. So, take a pre-frozen container with a big surface area and put the newly frozen ice cream in there and straight into the freezer. Avoid opening the freezer until it is properly frozen.

Structure

Now that you have a bit of background information on ingredients and manufacturing, we can look at things in more detail on a structural level.

Ice cream is a complex food colloid composed of air bubbles covered with fat globules and proteins, ice crystals, and an unfrozen water phase containing proteins, sugars, and other solids. Here is how this complex piece of art comes to live:

As mentioned earlier, we need to heat up our ingredients in order to melt all the fat and denature some proteins. The denatured proteins increase the viscosity of the ice cream, gives a richer mouth feeling and increases the air content. Having all the fat as liquid (because it has been melted) is important for the next step, homogenising. Homogenisation allows the liquid fat globules to separate out and we get a lot of smaller fat globules as you can see in figure 1.

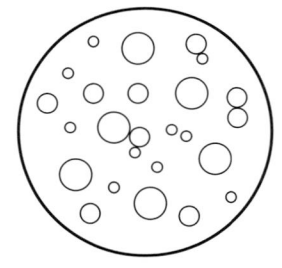

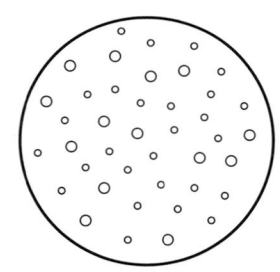

FIGURE 1. Bigger fat globules in a non-homogenised ice cream base (left) and smaller fat globules in a homogenised ice cream base (right). *Illustration courtesy of Prof. Douglas Goff, University of Guelph.*

When we have a lot of new fat globules, we have a lot more surface area of fat in the water phase. This means that we need some emulsifying components to lower the surface tension between these phases. Immediately after homogenising, the milk proteins casein and whey will adhere to the fat globular membrane and do the job as an emulsifier. This can be seen below in figure 2. The proteins are quite big and will create a thick membrane.

Fat globule without emulsifier

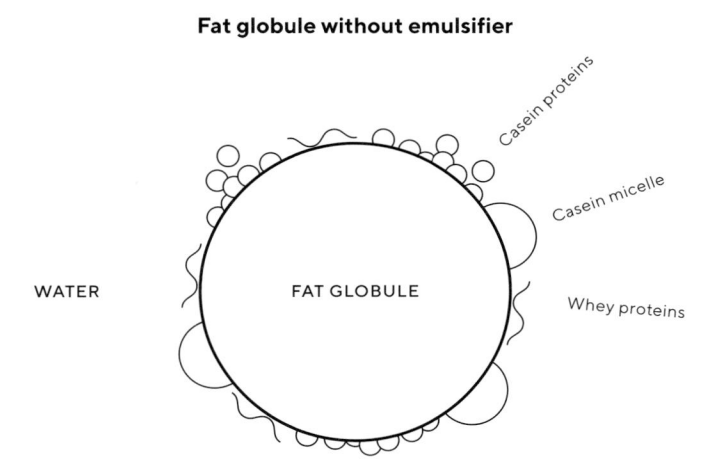

WATER — FAT GLOBULE — Casein proteins — Casein micelle — Whey proteins

FIGURE 2. Fat globule with milk protein on the fat globular membrane.
Illustration courtesy of Prof. Douglas Goff, University of Guelph.

When we leave the base to age for a minimum of 4 hours, the milk proteins are displaced from the fat globular membrane and the smaller molecular weight emulsifiers such as egg yolk phospholipids will, instead, adsorb to the membrane. This is illustrated in figure 3. As you can see, this creates a thinner membrane, which is beneficial once we start freezing and whipping our ice cream base. It is also beneficial to have more proteins enter into the water phase (the water phase already contains the different sugars, remaining proteins and stabilisers), because it increases the concentration and makes the water phase even more viscous. At the same time, ageing allows time for both the proteins and stabilisers to reach their full water binding capacity, again meaning an increased viscosity.

Last but not least: when we cool down the base during ageing, we allow some of the fat to solidify again but in, hopefully, smaller fat globules. This is beneficial for the freezing and whipping process.

Fat globule with emulsifier

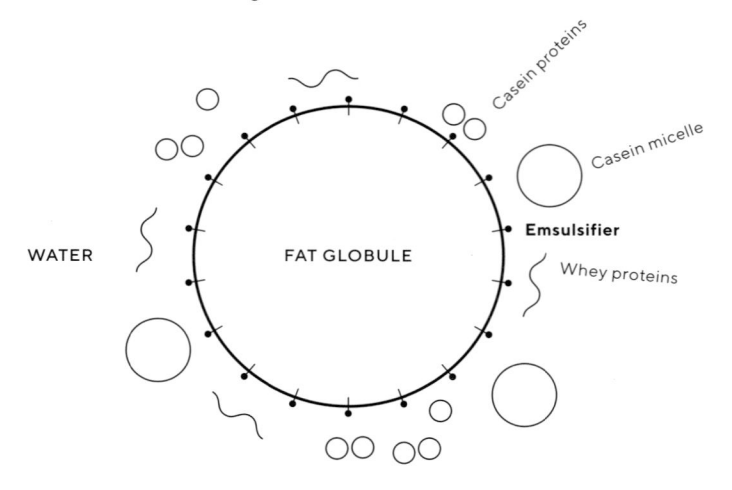

FIGURE 3. Fat globule after ageing with emulsifiers replacing the proteins on the fat globular membrane and some fat solidifying. *Illustration courtesy of Prof. Douglas Goff, University of Guelph.*

When we start freezing the ice cream there is continuous stirring and whipping taking place. This action results in a constant collision of the fat globules and adsorption to air bubbles. When the fat globules collide and stick to the surface of the air bubbles, they will hopefully generate the structure as can be seen in figure 4.

Fat globules destabilising

FIGURE 4. Fat globules partially coalescing as freezing and whipping is taking place. Ideal structure for adsorbing to air bubbles. *Illustration courtesy of Prof. Douglas Goff, University of Guelph.*

This happens because we have created a thinner membrane due to the replacement of milk proteins and some of the fat is solid and some is liquid, making it more ideal for creating this structure.

From figure 5 you can see the size of the fat globules in the base/mix (dotted line) and once it has been frozen into an ice cream the fat globules have collided and become destabilised (solid line). This means clusters have formed and they are measured to be bigger in size. If the fat globules are not destabilised adequately the below graph for the ice cream would look very similar to the graph for the base/mix as can be seen to the left – so the below to the right is the ideal picture.

Size of fat globules

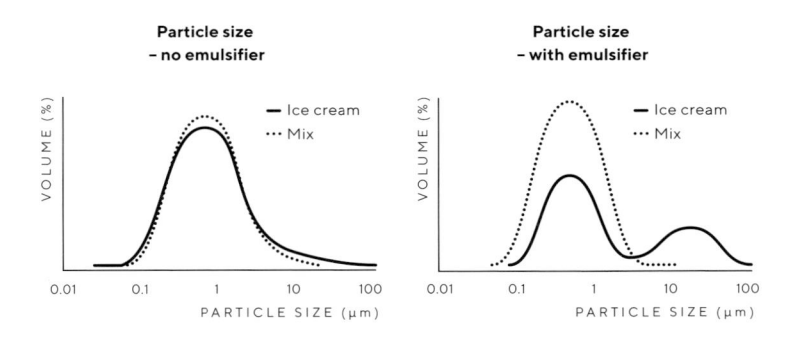

FIGURE 5. Particle size distribution in ice cream (solid line) and its base (dotted line) from light scattering spectroscopy. *Illustration courtesy of Prof. Douglas Goff, University of Guelph.*

This fat globular network is excellent for stabilising the air bubbles, which are also incorporated as the ice cream base is whipped. The amount of air that is incorporated depends on how well the structure of the fat globules is created, which again is dependent on the level and type of emulsifier and amount of fat present.

When the ice cream is freezing, the temperature is lowered, which means more and more water is turning into ice crystals. This is represented in

Figure 6. That means that there is less and less liquid water, which results in a water phase that becomes more and more concentrated with proteins, sugars, and stabilisers as the temperature is lowered. This solution can be considered a very viscous, almost gel like syrup. This solution does not freeze at a given temperature due to the addition of components that depress the freezing point.

Ice crystallisation

▽ Ice crystal   ∴ Mix

TEMPERATURE IS LOWERED ⟶

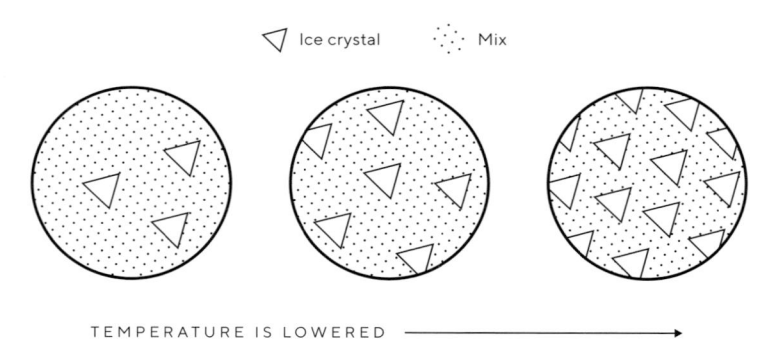

FIGURE 6. Increasing number of ice crystals are formed with decreasing temperatures. The remaining water phase becomes more concentrated as water freezes out of the solution. *Illustration courtesy of Prof. Douglas Goff, University of Guelph.*

The water phase only becomes more concentrated, and it will remain liquid, due to the FPDF. This is the reason an ice cream is scoopable: because there is liquid water left. At scooping temperatures of -15°C, approximately 60–80% of the water is in its solid shape as ice crystals and the remaining 20–40% is liquid water (the exact quantity depends on the amount and kind of sugars used).

Sugar & scoopability

As promised, here is your brief explanation to the sugar science and why the different kinds of sugars are used in the recipes, and how they affect the ice creams and sorbets.

I want to introduce two terms here: relative sweetness and Freezing Point Depression Factor (FPDF – this is one of my overall favourite terms in ice cream science! Purely because of how it sounds when you say it out loud). These are ways to measure how sweet a sugar is, and how much a sugar depresses the freezing point, respectively. To determine these values, sucrose is used as a reference point and therefore has a relative sweetness of 1 and a FPDF of 1.

Briefly, freezing point depression factor of a specific sugar is simply the molar weight ratio of this specific sugar to sucrose, that has a molecular weight of 342 g/mol. So, a rule of thumb is that monosaccharides have a higher FPDF due to the lower molecular weight. The relative sweetness is determined on a sensorical level.

TABLE 3. Relative sweetness and freezing point depression factor of different kinds of sugars and ethanol.

Sugar	Relative Sweetness	FPDF**
Sucrose	1.0	1.0
Glucose syrup solids (40–44 DE*)	0.3–0.5	0.8
Dextrose	0.7–0.8	1.9
Fructose	1.7	1.9
Lactose	0.2	1.0
Ethanol	0.0	6.9

* DE stands for dextrose equivalents. It is an index for how hydrolysed the glucose is.
The nomenclature of glucose and dextrose is actually very confusing when used in the ice cream industry, because dextrose=glucose. But we will not get too much into this here. Just accept it.

** FPDF: Freezing point depression factor

SOFTNESS

Softness of the three ice creams at −18°C

Base 3C Base 3B Base 3A

The values of different sugars have been determined with sucrose as the reference and are shown in table 3 for a few commonly used sugars together with values for alcohol (ethanol). In case you wanted to know.

If we for instance look at dextrose in table 3, we can see that dextrose has a relative sweetness of 0.7–0.8 and a FPDF of 1.9. This means that 1 g of dextrose is only 70–80% as sweet as 1 g of sucrose, where as it almost depresses the freezing point twice as much as sucrose (1.9 vs. 1.0), meaning the ice cream gets much softer at a given temperature than if sucrose was added.

On page 136 the scoopability is shown when we make a very soft ice cream (base 3A), a very hard ice cream (base 3B) and a standard ice cream recipe (base 3C) and serve them at -18°C.

Another little piece of sugar information: sweetness is perceived best around body temperature, and the lower the temperature the less sweet the ice cream or sorbet will be perceived. This practically means that when you sample your unfrozen mix, it needs to be a bit sweeter than you actually want the finished, frozen product to be.

Want to know

If you too are captivated by the world of ice cream science, I have collected a few points that you might want to know. If not, too bad.

STORING ICE CREAM AND SHELF LIFE

I am often asked what the shelf life of our ice cream is. I reply back with a smile: "At which temperature do you store it and are you referring to quality or microbiology?". The reason for this is that the shelf life of an ice cream depends on the storage temperature. And from a microbiological point of view, there are usually no problems at -18°C or colder.

If you recall what you have (hopefully) learnt about solid and liquid water in an ice cream, you should know that the colder an ice cream is, the more solid water there is. A high amount of solid water means the structure is more stable and less prone to create big ice crystals because there is less liquid water moving around. So, a rule of thumb: the colder your storage freezer, the longer the shelf life. If you store your ice cream at -30°C, it can last for months or years. If you store your ice cream at -12°C we are talking days. And this is regarding the structural shelf life.

One of the worst things you can do to an ice cream or sorbet is to expose it to many different temperatures. Temperature fluctuations could occur if you take an ice cream container in and out of a freezer and into room temperatures. Every time this happens, some of the solid water melts and become liquid. When the ice cream is then frozen back down, this newly formed liquid water will refreeze, but it does this by adsorbing onto the existing ice crystals, hence the new ice crystals will be bigger and more noticeable in the mouth. Remember this if you buy an ice cream from the supermarket which is a bit icy: it would probably have been extremely smooth and creamy coming out of the factory, but who knows what had happened during distribution? So do not blame the ice cream brand – blame the people handling the ice cream inadequately.

WORKING WITH ICE CREAM

Avoid using a hot spoon or hot knife if you plan on storing your ice cream after scooping or cutting. Using hot utensils will melt the ice cream surrounding the hot utensil, which means that the layer around the utensil will

MELTDOWN STABILITY TEST

Base 1 with whole eggs

Base 2 without egg yolks

Base 2 with egg yolks

0 minutes　　　　　　　　15 minutes　　　　　　　　30 minutes

turn icy when it is frozen down again. If you are consuming it right away, this will not be a problem.

If you want to wash your spoon/knife in warm water, just make sure there is no water left on the utensil, as this will turn into frozen ice droplets on the scoop or cake.

ICE CRYSTALS The ice crystals created from external water drops on the ice cream are very big compared to the ice crystals in the ice cream created from temperature fluctuations or ice crystals generated from a slow freezing cycle. So, if someone is complaining about ice crystals you actually have to ask: "what kind of ice crystals are you talking about?" As weird as it may sound, answering this question is part of my training protocol in working with ice creams.

WATCHING ICE CREAM MELT "You can learn a lot from watching ice cream melt".
— Professor Douglas Goff, University of Guelph, December 2014

I was told this by my ice cream Professor Dr. Douglas Goff, from University of Guelph when I attended his ice cream technology course for the first time in 2014. I was working on my master thesis, and when I first heard this, I thought that was a very odd thing to say. Little did I know, I had 26 hours ahead of me, where I would look at my 48 different ice cream samples melt for two hours*. Every 10 minute I had to register the amount of liquid that had dripped off and then take a picture. Trust me when I say, Dr. Goff was right: there is a huge difference in how ice cream melts.

Even now, when I go out to try other ice cream brands with my friends, I like to leave 3⁄4 of the ice cream and watch it melt; it tells you so much about the ingredients and the manufacturing, which is super exciting information to obtain.

A side note: I also learned I have to warn my friends about this before we go out for ice cream. Apparently not everyone enjoys this "watching-ice-cream-melt"-game as much as I do…

---

* I could only measure 4 at a time and I had to redo 2 batches, hence the 26 hours.

140 WANT TO KNOW

If you are not convinced yet, just look at the image on page 139. Hopefully you understand what I mean and can see the same beauty of watching ice cream melt.

NOTES ON THE DECIMALS

IF you are one of the very nerdy types that is just super annoyed that I have used either no decimals or 1 decimal in this book, then please know it is totally on purpose. For instance, I really just want you to add 0.2% of locust bean gum and I really want you to understand how the 5.6% MSNF in cream is calculated. If I, for instance, just wrote 6% MSNF, it would hurt my little ice cream heart, because there is an equation to find out this value. But at the same time, I cannot guarantee you that the cream contains 38.0% fat instead of 38.1%. And yes, I know if there is a variety in the fat% it would influence the MSNF% – but not that much.

So, the use of decimals is very carefully selected, but not necessarily in the same way as a hardcore mathematician would have selected it. I guess that is why I became a creative ice cream girl instead of a full-time scientist.

SOME RECIPES ARE MISSING

… you might think to yourself. Like lemon sorbet, coconut ice cream, raspberry sorbet or mint with chocolate chips. I can only say that you make choices in life and sometimes that means missing out on a lot of other great things. Luckily, you now have the skills to try to make these yourself!

Index of recipes

Avocado & lime sorbet with dates	40	Mango & coconut palm syrup	85
Banana sorbet	82	Mangosteen sorbet	39
Base 1 (Cream)	18	Maple & walnut	68
Base 2 (Milk)	19	Matcha & white chocolate	35
Base 3 (Sugar specific)	20	Melting chocolate	112
Beer ice cream with peanut nougat	48	Nougat	97
Brownie	94	Nut paste	104
Buttermilk, vanilla & lemon	29	Olive oil	71
Cakes	114	Passionfruit & Earl Grey	55
Caramelised grapefruit sorbet	78	Pistachio	63
Caramelised white chocolate	35	Pumpkin spice	72
Cashew nut	64	Rhubarb sorbet	89
Cherry sorbet	81	Saffron & honey	75
Chocolate ice cream	33	Salty caramel	95
Chocolate sorbet	32	Salty caramel sauce	95
Cinnamon & white chocolate	35	Sea buckthorn sorbet	77
Cones	108	Sticks	111
Cookie dough	99	Strawberry	88
Cookies	102	Strawberry sorbet	89
Cucumber, mint & lime sorbet	36	Syrup 1 (Simple)	22
Drunk prunes	43	Syrup 2 (Stronger structure)	23
Elderflower sorbet	44	Syrup 3 (Sugar specific)	25
Espresso ice cream	47	Tonka bean	60
Fruit sauce	107	Vanilla	51
Gin & yuzu sorbet	39		
Ginger & chili	71		
Hazelnut	66		
Irish cream stracciatella	98		
Is-à-la-mande	52		
Jackfruit ice cream	55		
Kombucha sorbet	59		
Lavender nougat	56		
Liquorice	86		

Conversion table

For some reason you need to convert certain measurements, here is a standard conversion table.

TABLE 4. Weight conversions.
gram (g), kilogram (kg), ounce (oz), pounds (lbs)

Metric	US / UK
1 g	0.03527 oz
5 g	0.18 oz
10 g	0.35 oz
25 g	0.88 oz
50 g	1.76 oz
75 g	2.65 oz
100 g	3.5 oz
200 g	7.05 oz
300 g	10.58 oz
500 g	17.64 oz (1.10 lbs)
750 g	26.46 oz (1.65 lbs)
1000 g (1 kg)	35.27 oz (2.20 lbs)

TABLE 5. Weight conversions, particularly relevant for this book.

1 egg yolk	15–20 g
1 egg white	30–40 g
1 tsp locust bean gum	2 g

References & special thanks

Most of the knowledge from this book I "just know" after spending years researching and investigating ice creams and sorbets. But when I need to look up something and check if I am going in the right direction, I often turn to these sources. The first being a course manual with a really good description of everything you might need to know. The second is a book going through a lot of details in the field of ice cream science, and the latter being a scientific review where I can get a quick and precise overview – in case I forget it.

Goff, H.D., 2018, Ice cream technology short course manual, University of Guelph, Canada.
Goff, H. D. & Hartel, R.W., 2013, Ice Cream 7th ed., New York: Springer.
Goff, H.D., 1997, Colloidal aspects of ice cream – A review, International Dairy Journal, 7 (6-7), pp. 363–373.

Needless to say, I have the biggest respect for the work Professor Douglas Goff has conducted within the field of ice cream science and how much he has contributed to the general understanding of how an ice cream is composed. I am truly grateful for everything I have learned from him. Thank you!

SPECIAL THANKS TO

All of my incredible regular customers who make sure we as a team are always on our toes with new flavours and quality, and who support us and keep coming back for more ice cream (sometimes twice a day).

All of my amazing friends who have stuck around and are willing to hear about my ideas about this book and all my other ice cream adventures. I am happy you are still part of my life even though I cannot talk about anything else than ice cream most of the time.